Courthouses *of* Georgia

GEORGIA
HUMANITIES
COUNCIL

Published in association with the Georgia Humanities Council

The University of Georgia Press   *Athens & London*

Courthouses *of* Georgia

ASSOCIATION COUNTY COMMISSIONERS OF GEORGIA

PHOTOGRAPHS BY GREG NEWINGTON

FOREWORD BY ROSS KING

INTRODUCTION BY LARRY WALKER

TEXT BY GEORGE JUSTICE

© 2014 by the University of Georgia Press
Athens, Georgia 30602
www.ugapress.org
All rights reserved
Designed by Erin Kirk New
Set in Adobe Garamond Pro
Manufactured by Kings Time Printing Press
The paper in this book meets the guidelines for
permanence and durability of the Committee on
Production Guidelines for Book Longevity of the
Council on Library Resources.

Most University of Georgia Press titles are
available from popular e-book vendors.

Printed in China
18 17 16 15 14 c 5 4 3 2 1

Library of Congress Cataloging-in-Publication Data

Courthouses of Georgia / Association County
Commissioners of Georgia ; photographs by Greg
Newington ; foreword by Ross King ; introduction by
Larry Walker ; text by George Justice.
     pages cm
  Includes bibliographical references.
ISBN 978-0-8203-4688-5 (hardcover : alk. paper) —
ISBN 0-8203-4688-8 (hardcover : alk. paper)
  1. Courthouses--Georgia. I. Association County
Commissioners of Georgia.
  NA4472.G4C68   2014
  725'.1509758—dc23   2014005790

British Library Cataloging-in-Publication Data available

This book is dedicated to those individuals who have answered the call of public service and given of their time and talents for the betterment of their communities as an elected county official, county staff member, or volunteer.

Contents

Contents by County
xi

Foreword by
Ross King xiii

INTRODUCTION
Memories of
Georgia Courthouses,
by Larry Walker 1

―――――

Glossary of
Architectural Terms 345

A Note on the Text by
George Justice 347

Acknowledgments
349

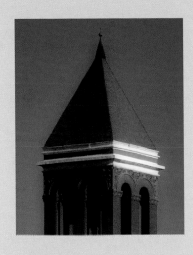

Historic
High County

9

Northeast
Georgia
Mountains

45

Atlanta
Metro

81

Presidential
Pathways

101

Historic
Heartland

141

Classic South

181

Plantation
Trace

217

Magnolia
Midlands

271

The Coast

321

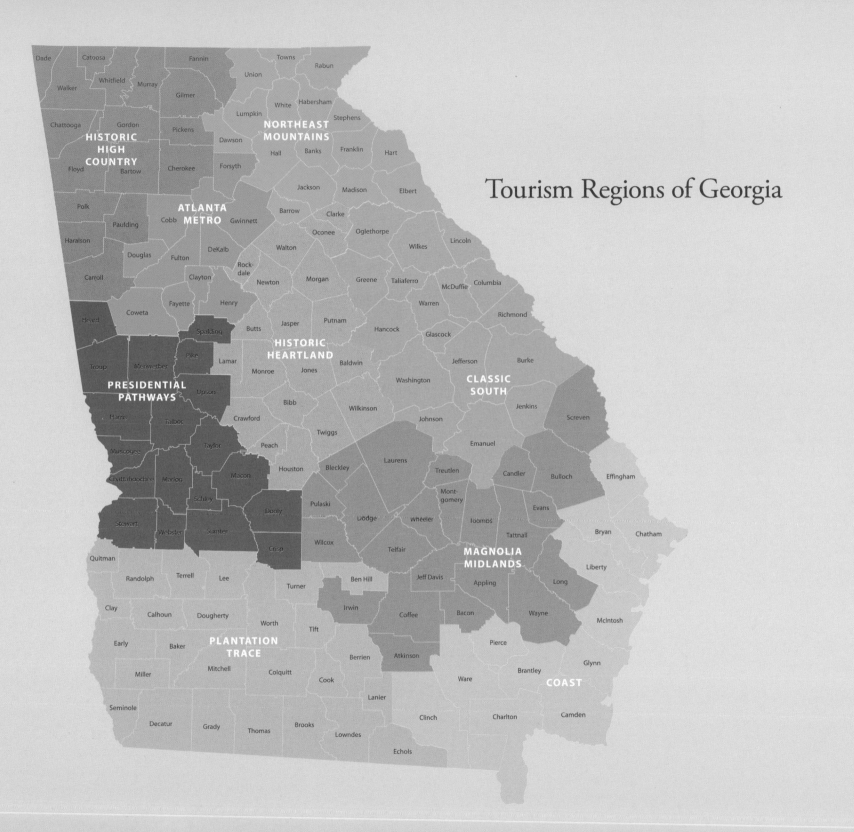

Tourism Regions of Georgia

CONTENTS BY COUNTY

Appling 272

Atkinson 274

Bacon 276

Baker 218

Baldwin 142

Banks 46

Barrow 48

Bartow 10

Ben Hill 278

Berrien 220

Bibb (Macon-Bibb County) 144

Bleckley 280

Brantley 322

Brooks 222

Bryan 324

Bulloch 282

Burke 182

Butts 146

Calhoun 224

Camden 326

Candler 284

Carroll 12

Catoosa 14

Charlton 328

Chatham 330

Chattahoochee (Cusseta-Chattahoochee County) 102

Chattooga 16

Cherokee 18

Clarke (Athens-Clarke County) 148

Clay 226

Clayton 82

Clinch 228

Cobb 84

Coffee 286

Colquitt 230

Columbia 184

Cook 232

Coweta 86

Crawford 150

Crisp 104

Dade 20

Dawson 50

Decatur 234

DeKalb 88

Dodge 288

Dooly 106

Dougherty 236

Douglas 90

Early 238

Echols (Echols County Consolidated Government) 240

Effingham 332

Elbert 52

Emanuel 186

Evans 290

Fannin 22

Fayette 92

Floyd 24

Forsyth 54

Franklin 56

Fulton 94

Gilmer 26

Glascock 188

Glynn 334

Gordon 28

Grady 242

Greene 190

Gwinnett 96

Habersham 58

Hall 60

Hancock 192

Haralson 30

Harris 108

Hart 62

Heard 110

Henry 98

Houston 152

Irwin 292

Jackson 64

Jasper 154

Jeff Davis 294

Jefferson 194

Jenkins 196

Johnson 198

Jones 156

Lamar 158

Lanier 244

Laurens 296

Lee 246

Liberty 336

Lincoln 200

Long 298

Lowndes 248

Lumpkin 66

Macon 112

Madison 68

Marion 114

McDuffie 202

McIntosh 338

Meriwether 116

Miller 250

Mitchell 252

Monroe 160

Montgomery 300

Morgan 162

Murray 32

Muscogee (Columbus-Muscogee County) 118

Newton 164

Oconee 166

Oglethorpe 204

Paulding 34

Peach 168

Pickens 36

Pierce 340

Pike 120

Polk 38

Pulaski 302

Putnam 170

Quitman (Georgetown–Quitman County) 254

Rabun 70

Randolph 256

Richmond (Augusta-Richmond County) 206

Rockdale 172

Schley 122

Screven 304

Seminole 258

Spalding 124

Stephens 72

Stewart 126

Sumter 128

Talbot 130

Taliaferro 208

Tattnall 306

Taylor 132

Telfair 308

Terrell 260

Thomas 262

Tift 264

Toombs 310

Towns 74

Treutlen 312

Troup 134

Turner 266

Twiggs 174

Union 76

Upson 136

Walker 40

Walton 176

Ware 342

Warren 210

Washington 212

Wayne 314

Webster (Unified Government of Webster County) 138

Wheeler 316

White 78

Whitfield 42

Wilcox 318

Wilkes 214

Wilkinson 178

Worth 268

FOREWORD   Ross King, Executive Director, Association County Commissioners of Georgia

Government has long been a fascination of mine. My father dedicated his professional career to the federal government. He served in various leadership positions for the Civil Service Commission and the Office of Personnel Management that concentrated on training senior-level federal employees. Our family moved several times over the years as his career progressed, giving me the opportunity to experience the natural beauty and cultural diversity of our great country.

In my seventh- and ninth-grade years, I enjoyed the dedication and commitment to civic engagement demonstrated by my junior and senior high instructors. They presented with passion and purpose the value of public service and the linkage of federal, state, and local governments. As a college student, I was naturally drawn to political science and public administration. While I was in graduate school, a professor responded to my extreme interest in civic engagement and encouraged me to explore an internship in the City of Americus in Sumter

County, Georgia, with Mayor Russell Thomas Jr. This experience not only led me to a lifelong mentor but also reaffirmed my public service calling and sparked an interest in historic preservation— especially for those buildings that are part of the heartbeat of our local communities.

During my tenure in Americus, the city was named a Georgia Main Street Community, created a downtown development authority, and established a twelve-block redevelopment initiative with the focal point being the preservation of the Windsor Hotel (built in 1892). This landmark still stands today as a lasting tribute to the area's past and a tourism draw for people from around the world.

In many of Georgia's counties, the historic courthouse is the central focus of the town square. Entire communities have emerged from where the cornerstones of these buildings were placed. Decades ago, that growth was often the direct result of the expansion of the state's transportation network, especially during the development of the rail system.

In more recent decades, it has been driven by other kinds of economic development. Yet one can still drive through many a county seat and get an immediate feel for the sense of community based on the area surrounding the courthouse.

Over the years, a number of historic courthouses have been lost to fires or have been torn down. Many others have been dramatically restored and protected as community treasures through designation on the National Register of Historic Places. Some courthouses built as far back as the late 1800s are still in use today, while other counties have built more modern justice centers to handle the expanding demands for county services and have transitioned their historic structures to county administrative offices, community centers, museums, and other uses. In every instance, the county courthouse provides a true sense of community!

ACCG, Georgia's county association, has chosen to pay tribute to our county courthouses through the publication of this photography book as part of our centennial anniversary. Formed in 1914 by county commissioners to help support the organization of the state's first highway department, today ACCG's membership includes all 159 Georgia counties. ACCG is one of the recognized national leaders among county associations as a result of efforts in advancing Georgia's counties through legislative advocacy, leadership development, civic engagement, and membership services programs designed to increase efficiencies and lower costs for county government operations.

Browse through the pages of this book and enjoy the stature and elegance of Georgia's county courthouses while learning about each building's general architecture and the origins of its county. To learn more, turn first to the New Georgia Encyclopedia. Developed as a program of the Georgia Humanities Council in partnership with the University of Georgia Press, the University System of Georgia / GALILEO, and the Office of the Governor, this online resource provides more in-depth information on significant people, places, and events that shaped our state.

Find your county's courthouse, or the courthouses in the communities where you or members of your family have lived. Better yet, spend time using this book as a travel guide to explore various regions of the state. They say that a picture is worth a thousand words, and photographer Greg Newington has certainly captured the spirit of these courthouses with his remarkable artistic style. However, as someone who has traveled this state for more than three decades and has stood in front of or walked the halls of nearly all of these courthouses, I can attest that they are worth the trip.

Courthouses *of* Georgia

INTRODUCTION *Memories of Georgia Courthouses* Larry Walker

Falsely promising to block the way, the monumental building rises straight ahead. Tall and wide, with white wooden lace falling over rich red brick as its high windows point toward the bright white of the cupola crown, this is the law's palace. Georgia's grandiloquent courthouses are her architectural glory. Creaking majesty may be a lot for a worn-down town to carry, but whether, as here in Sparta, in splendid raiment or where prosperity has forced the law to don drab modern garb, the courthouse reigns in each of the state's 159 counties.
—William S. McFeely, *Proximity to Death*

The grand Houston County Courthouse, erected on the square in downtown Perry in 1855 to replace an earlier frame courthouse on the same site, provides my earliest memory of a county courthouse. Let me explain.

The image in my mind of how the building looked largely comes from a vintage postcard photo that hangs in my law office. It appears that the photographer shot the picture from the northwest to the southeast showing the old building as it fronted on Carroll and Ball Streets.

The main facade of the courthouse has nine windows and an entrance that is basically at ground level, with a slight upward slope to the door. The building is surrounded by trees. I recall that a giant magnolia stood on the site at its northeast corner; the tree remained long after the building was razed. This magnolia, likely a favorite gathering place of old men, is not shown in my photograph. My aunt, Virginia Gray Mason, now ninety-five years of age, tells me that "back then" a gazebo on the courthouse grounds was used by bands and singing

groups and for other celebrations and gatherings. The photo also shows that there was a covered well on the grounds, a place to get a drink and to water the mules and horses, I suppose.

The hip-roofed building, as best as I can tell from my black-and-white photograph, was of red brick construction, its wooden trim painted white.

But I have a remembrance beyond this one. Some additional knowledge was gleaned from a trip I made with my grandfather Gray to the courthouse when I was five or six years old. This would have been 1947 or '48, just shortly before the building was destroyed.

I remember nothing from the trip about the building's appearance—what I do remember, vividly to this day, is how the courthouse smelled. The very walls of the old building seemed saturated with a distinctive odor, ninety-plus years in the making. A smell so distinctive that one doesn't forget it, even if it was over sixty years ago.

The courthouse, back in those days, was largely the province of old men. When they could no longer farm or do other work, many made the courthouse their place of social intercourse. And there they were, in their well-worn work clothes—wool pants and wool hats in the winter, denim in the summer—and with their tobacco and spittoons. The building was probably coal- or wood-heated in cold weather and fully open in summer. So, what I remember, and always will, was the odor that was a part of the warp and woof of the building.

There is a third part that completes my image of the building, and that is the tales from those I loved and respected about what took place in that structure. And no story is more ingrained in me than that of the murder trial of Thomas G. Woolfolk in the late 1800s.

The Woolfolk case, originally a Bibb County case tried there three times, but transferred to Houston County as the result of a change-of-venue request because of the inability to get a fair trial in Bibb, arose from Woolfolk being accused of bludgeoning to death nine of his family members, ranging in age from eighty-four years to eighteen months and including his father and stepmother, all with his father's short-handled ax.

Bloody Woolfolk, as he was dubbed in the press, was incarcerated in Houston County in what is now Walker-Rhodes Tractor Co., a building presently owned by my family. Evidence of its jail heritage are bars on some of the back windows and shards

of glass still imbedded in the walls protruding above the roof, ostensibly to keep prisoners such as Woolfolk from escaping via a roof exit.

This was a murder and trial of national interest. Songs were written about Tom Woolfolk and his heinous acts of August 6, 1887. It was not until June 25, 1889, in the Houston County Courthouse, that Woolfolk was properly convicted with his sentence to be hanged by the neck until dead. Bloody Woolfolk was hanged the following September in Perry at the confluence of Big Indian Creek and Fanny Gresham Branch, and in sight of Evergreen Cemetery. Bobbe Smith Hickson, in her book *A Land So Dedicated*, called the Woolfolk murders "the most notorious court case of the century." Legend has it that upward of ten thousand citizens showed up to see Tom Woolfolk on the gallows.

It's the tales and the smells and a long-ago photo snapped for a postcard that binds me to Houston County's second courthouse.

And then there was in 1950, on the same Perry town square, the new courthouse. It was two stories high, with a basement and constructed of gray satin-finished bricks. A county official said on the occasion of its dedication that the building would be "adequate for the county for at least the next fifty years." It was supposedly paid for, in full, all $325,000.00 for its 22,250 square feet, when the doors opened for county business.

How prophetic was the official who predicted fifty years of active service as a courthouse (although additional government facilities had been built in

Warner Robins, by the time this building became just another government structure and not a courthouse) before a new behemoth building of 112,400 square feet on the outskirts of Perry was dedicated in 2002 as the county courthouse. This is the third Houston County Courthouse of which I have memories, and at least the fourth in the county's history.

Today, the refurbished 1950 building on the square makes do as a voter registration office, polling place, and venue for agricultural education. But it has a storied and glorious past worthy of remembrance. Let me share some of my personal connections and memories with you.

It's where I tried my first court case. The case involved a dispute between two men who were raising quail in a partnership when one accused the other of theft by converting the birds to use as food (fried, I assume, and probably with grits) and filed a civil lawsuit against the man would be my first client.

The quail case was tried before a jury, and I made my first closing argument calling the case "one for the birds"—and got my first favorable jury verdict.

This courthouse is the one in which Sam Nunn practiced law. It was in the clerk's record room of this courthouse that I introduced a smiling gubernatorial candidate, Jimmy Carter, to a serious lawyer, Sam Nunn, never imagining that I was introducing a future president of the United States to a future U.S. senator.

Willis Hunt, later to be a Superior Court judge, chief justice of the Georgia Supreme Court, and a federal district court judge, practiced law in this courthouse. Hunt would likely call this building his home courthouse. Many other great lawyers and judges, too numerous to mention, did good work on the square in Perry and in that courthouse.

So much history. And yet in the courtrooms of this courthouse, nothing was as eerily similar to the old courthouse and the 1889 Woolfolk murder trial as the 1988 retrial of Carl Isaacs, the accused ringleader of a mass murder in Seminole County in 1973. The presiding judge was the specially appointed Superior Court Judge Hugh Lawson, then a Federal District Court judge in the Middle District of Georgia.

In Lawson's words:

Courthouses have been the scenes of some of society's greatest public dramas—criminal jury trials. Every county has its favorite story to tell but some are more compelling than others. One of the most notorious in our time was the 1973 trial of Carl Isaacs, one of the infamous killers of six members of the Alday family in Seminole County. At the time then Governor Jimmy Carter called the murders "the most heinous crime in Georgia."

The trial was held in Perry because of a court-ordered change of venue, it having been determined that Isaacs could not receive a fair trial in Donalsonville. When counsel for the state and

defendant could not agree on a location for the trial, the Houston County Courthouse in Perry was designated by the trial judge as the site of the trial.

The trial was held and Isaacs was found guilty of the six murders and sentenced to death. The verdict was affirmed by the Supreme Court of Georgia and the 11th Circuit Court of Appeals and the Supreme Court of the United Stated refused to hear a further appeal. Isaacs was executed at the state prison in Butts County on May 6, 2003, fifteen years after his final conviction and thirty years after the murders of five Alday men—Ned, Chester, Aubrey, Jimmy, and Jerry—and Jerry's pregnant wife, Mary.

Let's see what several other prominent Georgians say about our state's courthouses. First is William H. "Dink" NeSmith Jr., president of Athens-based Community Newspapers, who, like McFeely, writes of the appearance of the courthouse.

If I am driving through a town for the first time, I like to make a lap around the courthouse. The appearance of the structure says something.

Years ago, I stopped in Baxley to fill my gas tank. The service station attendant pointed to the construction activity across the street. "That's a waste of tax-payers' money," he fumed. "That old courthouse ain't worth fixing up."

A few years later, I pulled back into the same station for another fill-up. The same fellow greeted me. This time, I pointed to the building across the street. Before I could say anything, he piped up: "Doesn't it look great? We're really proud of our courthouse."

We are warned by proverb not to judge a book by its cover. Still, when I see a courthouse that's begging for repair, I form an opinion: this is a community begging for someone to care.

A pen-and-ink drawing of my hometown's courthouse hangs over my desk. Even though I now live 210 miles from Jesup, the Wayne County courthouse speaks to me every time I walk into my office. Huey Theus's artwork was done in 2002, just after the then 100-year-old courthouse was returned to its original glory. Inmates did much of the renovation. Many of them were found guilty in the very courtroom they helped to restore.

Talk about a novel way to pay for your crime. I like what that says, too.

To Federal District Court judge, Northern District of Georgia, and a man who presided over many trials as a Superior Court judge, Steve Jones, it's memories and experiences and how the Athens–Clarke County Courthouse has impacted his life.

The Athens–Clarke County courthouse will always hold a special place in my heart as the place of a number of "firsts" for me—my first swearing in, my first jury trial, and my first time on the bench. In 1978, I began working at the courthouse, located in my home-town of Athens, as a non-lawyer employee of the Child Support Recovery Unit. Through my work at the courthouse, I later decided that I wanted to become a lawyer. In 1987, I passed the bar and was sworn in as a lawyer at the courthouse. I went on to try my first case at the Athens–Clarke County courthouse, as an assistant district attorney. In 1995, I became a Superior Court judge and presided over my first jury trial—and later thousands of other cases—at the Athens–Clarke County courthouse.

I know the ins and outs of the Athens–Clarke County courthouse and if its walls could talk, they would have a lot to tell. It has seen people at their best and at their worst. It is also the heart of the county because at some point in every Athenian's lifetime, he or she will have to come to the courthouse—whether it's for jury service, to obtain a marriage license, to pay a tax bill, or to appear in court for various reasons.

George Hooks, a multiple-term member of the Georgia General Assembly, and for many years the unofficial State Senate historian, probably has more intimate knowledge of Georgia courthouses than any living Georgian, as when he retired in 2012, he was representing eighteen counties with eighteen courthouses. George has particularly strong memories of two of "his" courthouses.

Marion County, created in December 1827, is unique among Georgia counties in that it has two standing courthouses, each with a state historical marker: one is titled the "Old" and the other the "New" courthouse.

The "Old" two-story frame courthouse was built between 1846 and 1848 in the tiny community of Tazwell for the tidy sum of $1,637. Shortly thereafter the locals voted to move the seat of government to the exact center of the county. The relocated county seat was named Buena Vista for the American victory in the Mexican War. In the spring of 1850, the "New" courthouse was completed with locally manufactured brick and mortar. It sits in the center of the town square, in the exact center of the county, and is a fine example of Greek Revival symmetry with four sets of Doric columns on each of the four sides.

The courthouses of Sumter, Dooly, Lee, and Macon counties contain the marriage license, probated will, and estate inventories of my forebears. However, in the new Marion County courthouse, my family can find these details back to the death of my fourth great-grandmother, who was buried under Marion County soil on November 28, 1838.

Webster County was created on December 16, 1853, as Kinchafoonee County. A legislative act on three years later changed the name to Webster, in honor of Whig Party leader U.S. Senator Daniel Webster and his role in the Compromise of 1850.

The grounds of the courthouse in the tiny county seat of Preston as much as the 1915 courthouse itself are significant in Georgia history. It was on this courthouse square, in the 1870s that a jury sentenced the first female to the gallows, for poisoning her husband before running off with a local minister. The trial became so infamous and news stories so widespread that the solicitor of the Southwestern Circuit (now District Attorney), Charles F. Crisp of Schley County, was elected to Congress, later becoming the Speaker of the U.S. House of Representatives.

It was on this courthouse square that a sixteen-year-old farm boy rode a mule, bareback, into town, gave a forty-minute speech on the "Duties of a Citizen" about Robert E. Lee, that he had committed to memory on Confederate Memorial Day in 1894. The young lad went on to law school at Mercer University and in 1922 was elected to the U.S. Senate from Georgia, and ultimately becoming president pro tempore of that body. The law school at Mercer University today bears his name: Walter F. George.

One who has distinguished herself at both the trial court level, as a Superior Court judge, and the appellate court level, as chief justice of that court, talks here about the courtroom of the Georgia Supreme Court. Many would echo Justice Carol Hunstein's words in describing other courthouses and courtrooms of the state.

Whenever I step into our courtroom, I am struck by its majesty as a solemn, sacred place. It is not old and musty, nor is it new and sterile. Rather it is stately and beautiful, as Georgia's highest court should be, with mahogany-paneled walls and burgundy-and-gold curtains. And as I listen to lawyers argue cases, I cannot help but be reminded that history permeates the place. More than a dozen portraits of justices who have come before us adorn our walls, as if stationed as sentries to ensure that justice will be done. I like to think they would approve and are satisfied that Georgia's Supreme Court forever embodies the words etched in white marble above our bench: "Let Justice Be Done, Though the Heavens May Fall."

Buddy DeLoach, a former mayor of Hinesville and a ten-year member of the Georgia House of Representatives, has his own "courthouse memories."

I started shining shoes in the Liberty County Courthouse the summer after I turned ten years old. I can still remember the combination of smells of tobacco smoke, spittoons, and freshly oiled floors. The men who occupied that building were all larger than life to me. I watched closely as they played jokes on one another and talked of past and coming elections. I learned about the pecking orders, heard them fuss with one another, and watched them close ranks when one came under attack from the outside. When people talked about the "courthouse gang," I thought I was a part of it.

There was an air of mystery about that building. Even at ten years old I understood that things happened there that changed lives.

The Liberty County Courthouse was the center of our community. As teenagers we drove around the square on warm summer nights in search of something that we could not explain.

We have a new Justice Center in Hinesville that is a beautiful building, but the old courthouse is more than a building. It is memories of the people and events that changed lives.

Bryant Culpepper practiced law in Fort Valley for many years, during which he also served eight years in the Georgia House of Representatives. Later he followed his father, Superior Court Judge George B. Culpepper III, to the post of Superior Court judge in the Macon Circuit, serving there for twenty-five years. He now practices in Macon.

Where does justice begin? Where does it come from? How does it arrive?

We often seek justice out of anger and retribution. Your eye for my eye. Your tooth for my tooth. Unchecked retaliation is not justice.

We seek justice because we also seek peace. There can be no peace without justice.

As this state grew and counties were formed, courthouses were built. Some were rough and ugly and some were palaces. All had the same purpose. All were built with the aspiration of the furtherance and maintenance of justice within the county boundaries.

The men, and later women, who served as judges, lawyers, sheriffs, bailiffs, and jurors were and still are charged with and obligated to simply be fair and just. We claim no greater right than the right to have a jury of fair people stand between us and our government.

There is nothing easy about justice. It is not dispensed from a tap like water. It is not free like air. But to the human soul, it's just as vital.

Justice comes only later if it comes at all. It comes after hard work. It comes after preparation. It comes in the desire to see a wrong corrected. It comes in light and never in darkness. It comes in affirmation of the truth.

It comes to us as a gift of God. It most often comes to us in a courthouse.

Southern culture is a storytelling culture. From our courthouses come some of the great storytellers in Georgia. Superior Court Judge Marion T. Pope (later a judge on the Court of Appeals) from Cherokee County, Superior Court Judge Lawton Stephens from Clarke County, Superior Court Judge

George Nunn from Houston County, and the great trial lawyer Hugh B. McNatt from Toombs County come to mind. But, none are better than that outstanding trial lawyer and former Georgia governor, Roy Eugene Barnes:

I love every courthouse in Georgia. It is where the business of the people is transacted in public view and gives transparency and confidence to all citizens.

One of my favorite courthouses, besides my home courthouse of Cobb County, is the historic courthouse in Walton County. I tried cases there years ago when it was in disrepair and there was an undertaking in the mid-1990s to restore the Walton County Courthouse. I was pleased to try the first jury trial in the restored courthouse. Although I lost the case, I enjoyed the old courthouse made new and restored to its former grandeur.

Another courthouse in which I always enjoyed trying cases was the old courthouse in Bartow County. It was a huge courtroom with a floor that sloped towards the bar of the court. In years past there was no air conditioning in the old courthouse and the windows were left open during summer months to get a little ventilation; the judge there would not allow the lawyers to remove their coats regardless of how hot and muggy it was. I remember during a closing argument a pigeon flew in the open window and relieved himself right in front of me while I spoke. It certainly broke the concentration of both me and the jury.

One of the things I have noticed is that in many courthouses, particularly north of the fall line, the jury box is directly in front of the judge rather than to the side. This was always disconcerting to me as I could not see what kind of expression the judge was making to the jury as my back was to the judge while I argued. I always worried that the jury looked to the judge for his reaction more than listening to my closing arguments.

One last remembrance is the old courthouse in Effingham County before it became a suburban county.

I went to try a civil case there (the only one on the calendar) and because I arrived at the courthouse quite early I passed the time by helping the bailiff sweep out the courtroom. The bench was extremely high in the old courthouse, and I asked some of the local folks why the bench was so high. They told me the story that the settlers of that county were very independent, and the judge told the county commissioner to lower the bench, as it was too high. In an act of defiance, the county commissioner instead raised the bench even higher.

And, lastly, we have the words of a great Georgia lawyer, Chuck Byrd, himself the son of a great Georgia lawyer and a former lieutenant governor of Georgia.

Travel around Georgia, find some of the old courthouses, walk around them, go inside, into the courtroom, look up to the judge's bench, sit at the lawyer's table, imagine a jury in the box, then turn around and look up to the balcony.

It seems like yesterday. My friends and I left school. We ran to the courthouse as fast as we could. The courtroom was packed. We quietly walked up the steps into the balcony and squeezed into the few remaining vacant seats. From there, I could see everything.

Even a half a century later, I can close my eyes and hear my father, Garland T. Byrd, argue that case to a Taylor County jury.

In *To Kill a Mockingbird*, Scout, Jem, and Dill, during Tom Robinson's trial, sat in the balcony with the Reverend Sykes. The balcony was where Reverend Sykes and other African Americans were required by Jim Crow to sit.

From that balcony, Scout and Jem could see everything. They could hear their father, Atticus Finch, try that case. In her book, Harper Lee placed those white children in that racially segregated balcony for a purpose. From that balcony, the children saw and heard their father seek justice. From that balcony, the children witnessed both the best and worst of American justice.

The courthouses of the state of Georgia stand as monuments to the best and worst in all of us.

As Martin Luther King said, "The arc of the moral universe is long, but it bends toward justice."

The ardent and eloquent words of several great Georgians with their memories and thoughts of what courthouses have meant to them and of how the institutions housed therein have impacted the lives of their family, friends, and fellow Georgians.

And, yet, with these Georgians, plus my own courthouse memories, only a few courthouses have been mentioned by name. There are so many more. The 159 Georgia counties and the memories of literally millions of Georgians about these county buildings live through what has taken place inside their almost hallowed walls.

What takes place in our courthouses is determined by the usual and primary elected occupants of these courthouses, both large and small, rural and urban. It's our sheriffs, clerks of court, probate judges, tax commissioners, Superior Court judges, and district attorneys. But, here, and for this book, let us briefly examine the role of those in the legislative branch of county government, our county commissioners.

Georgia's county commissioners, for well over one hundred years, have been at the frontlines of Georgia politics. Many have helped spawn county political organizations. They prospered under Georgia's county unit system, and today they effectively carry out the people's business with laptops on the meeting room table. These officials, formally Commissioners of Roads and Revenues, exemplify the best of representative democracy. And they, when needed—often with great political courage and with the specter of their own political demise at the forefront—have replaced old courthouses with new.

Our courthouses are where our county commissioners meet and determine questions of taxation. It's where decisions are made about where roads will be built and when they will be repaired. The court house is the official gathering place for these officials who have counted among their numbers some of the most colorful and capable politicians and public servants in the history of Georgia.

In these brief remarks, both Judge Steve Jones and Chuck Byrd have written that the state's 159 courthouses symbolize the best and worst of our people. That is so true. The courthouse is where couples are married and where divorces are granted. It's where bought land is registered and where lawsuits over "family inherited land" are settled. It's where one gets a gun permit and it's where murder trials are held. When there is a birth, a record is made, and when there is a death someone registers that also, often in the same office. The courthouse is where one pays taxes and where one might be ordered to pay other debts to society.

That the Georgia courthouse represents the best and worst at the same time is probably based on our heritage. It's the Confederate monument on the courthouse square with words like those on the statute at the 1950 courthouse in downtown Perry: "May This Shaft Ever Call to Memory the Story of the Glory of the Men Who Wore the Gray." For some that's "the best," and to others that's "the worst."

This is what this book is all about. It's for us to look, see, and remember: memories good and bad, history laudable and shameful. Despite our many and different memories, most will rightfully conclude that virtually no other civic structure affects Georgians as much these buildings, Georgia's 159 courthouses.

Historic High Country

Bartow County

ADDRESS
115 West Cherokee Avenue
Cartersville, Georgia 30120

YEAR COMPLETED
1903

ARCHITECTURAL STYLE
Neoclassical Revival

DESIGNER
Kenneth McDonald and J. W. Golucke

MATERIAL
Brick

YEAR PLACED ON NATIONAL REGISTER
OF HISTORIC PLACES
1980

CURRENT USE
Courthouse / Multipurpose

Legend has it that the county commissioned the building of a new Bartow County courthouse in 1902 because the previous structure was too close to the railroad tracks. Located in Cartersville, the main entrance of the courthouse features a portico with six columns under a pediment. There also is a balcony on the second floor that stretches the length of the portico. The octagonal pedestal supporting the broad clock tower has pediments around the arched belfry. A golden dome with clocks in all directions sits on the tower and adds additional detail.

Bartow County was created from Cherokee County in 1832. It was originally named Cass County to honor General Lewis Cass, secretary of war under President Andrew Jackson. It was renamed in 1861 for General Francis S. Bartow, the first Georgia officer to fall at the First Battle of Manassas.

Carroll County

ADDRESS
323 Newnan Street
Carrollton, Georgia 30117

YEAR COMPLETED
1928

ARCHITECTURAL STYLE
Italian Renaissance Revival

DESIGNER
William J. J. Chase

MATERIAL
Stone

YEAR PLACED ON NATIONAL REGISTER
OF HISTORIC PLACES
1980

CURRENT USE
County Commission and
Administrative Offices

The historic Carroll County courthouse in Carrollton contains the largest courtroom in Georgia, covering 3,200 square feet with a 25-foot-high ceiling. Just beyond the balustrades at the main entrance is the front door with a beautifully crafted pediment and clock insert. Across the second-story are four column pilasters spaced to frame the three large arched windows of the courtroom. Two elegant medallions on the second story have etchings of Blind Justice sitting with her scales.

Carroll County was created by an act of the state legislature in 1825. All of the territory provided for the county had been Creek Indian land ceded by the 1825 Treaty of Indian Springs. The county is named for Charles Carroll of Maryland, who at the time was the last surviving signer of the Declaration of Independence.

Catoosa County

7694 Nashville Street
Ringgold, Georgia 30736

YEAR COMPLETED
1939

ARCHITECTURAL STYLE
Colonial Revival

DESIGNER
Crutchfield & Law

MATERIAL
Brick

YEAR PLACED ON NATIONAL REGISTER
OF HISTORIC PLACES
2006

CURRENT USE
Courthouse

The Public Works Administration built the Catoosa County courthouse in Ringgold during the Great Depression. The main entrance has an elegant design with an ornamental door framed with double-column pilasters. The scroll pediment, arched brick relief, and entrance pediment above the main door are other notable additions. There is a modest tower on the crest of the roof with a distinctive spire.

Catoosa County was originally part of Walker and Whitfield counties. Designated in 1853, its name reflects a prominent landmark, Catoosa Springs, which was named for a Cherokee Indian chief.

Chattooga County

ADDRESS
10035 Commerce Square
Summerville, Georgia 30747

YEAR COMPLETED
1909

ARCHITECTURAL STYLE
Neoclassical Revival

DESIGNER
Bryan Architectural Firm

MATERIAL
Concrete Block

YEAR PLACED ON NATIONAL REGISTER
OF HISTORIC PLACES
1980

CURRENT USE
Courthouse

The Chattooga County courthouse located in Summerville stands out against the backdrop of this ridge-and-valley region of northwest Georgia. This courthouse has a neoclassical design with four-columned porticos and handsome pediments with ornate reliefs. The octagonal clock tower is accented by a golden dome and cupola. The courthouse also has a stained-glass window depicting the seal of Georgia.

Chattooga County was created in 1838 from parts of Walker and Floyd counties by the state legislature. It is named for the Chattooga River.

Cherokee County

ADDRESS
100 North Street
Canton, Georgia 30114

YEAR COMPLETED
1929

ARCHITECTURAL STYLE
Stripped Classical

DESIGNER
A. Ten Eyck Brown

MATERIAL
Marble

YEAR PLACED ON NATIONAL REGISTER
OF HISTORIC PLACES
1981

CURRENT USE
County Offices and the Historical Society

The historic Cherokee County courthouse (pictured) in Canton has a number of distinctive characteristics. Four slender columns open into a small plaza that leads to the main entrance of this white marble building. The columns support a lintel that holds four sculpted American eagles. A stylish pediment hangs over the double wooden door on the plaza. A marble seal on the center of the facade has "1927" etched in it, indicating the year that the county approved the construction of this courthouse. In 1994, Cherokee County opened a new justice center. This facility, along with the historic courthouse and county administrative office, create a government complex in downtown Canton.

Cherokee County was created by legislative act in 1831 after the discovery of gold in the region. The area for the county came from territory previously held by the Cherokee Nation, which is the namesake for the county. In 1832, the land was divided into ten counties.

Dade County

12371 South Main Street
Trenton, Georgia 30752

YEAR COMPLETED
1926

ARCHITECTURAL STYLE
Vernacular (Dutch Colonial
Revival Influences)

DESIGNER
Barrett Construction Company

MATERIAL
Brick

YEAR PLACED ON NATIONAL REGISTER
OF HISTORIC PLACES
1980

CURRENT USE
Historic Courthouse / Tourism

The Dade County courthouse located in Trenton has a rectangular shape creating a simple symmetry. The main entrances have scrolled parapets with a small broken pediment at their peak. The pilasters beside the entrances have turret features that taper along the courthouse windows of the second story. All of the windows have decorative lintels. The inflated brick corners add further interest to this building's design.

In 1837, the state legislature created Dade County from western Walker County. The county name honors Major Francis Langhorne Dade, a Virginian who died in the Second Seminole War in Florida.

Fannin County

ADDRESS
400 West Main Street
Blue Ridge, Georgia 30513

YEAR COMPLETED
2004

ARCHITECTURAL STYLE
Modern

DESIGNER
Bruce Jennings

MATERIAL
Brick

CURRENT USE
Courthouse

The Appalachian Mountains offer a striking setting for two courthouses that sit side by side in Fannin County. Built in 2004, the present-day courthouse (pictured) blends elements of modern and traditional designs by including neoclassical features such as four white columns at the main entrance. The historic courthouse just behind the modern courthouse was built in 1937. This courthouse was designed in a late neoclassical style with the familiar portico, four columns, and an ornate pediment.

Fannin County was created in 1854 from parts of Gilmer and Union counties. The name honors Georgia native Colonel James W. Fannin. During the Texas Revolution, Fannin led 342 men who were captured and executed at the Battle of Goliad in 1836.

Floyd County

ADDRESS
4 Government Plaza
Rome, Georgia 30161

YEAR COMPLETED
1893

ARCHITECTURAL STYLE
Romanesque Revival

DESIGNER
Bruce & Morgan

MATERIAL
Brick

YEAR PLACED ON NATIONAL REGISTER
OF HISTORIC PLACES
1980

CURRENT USE
Offices of the Tax Assessor and
Tax Commissioner

Floyd County has three courthouses that are still in use today for a variety of county purposes. The oldest of the three (pictured) was built in 1893 and has a clock tower with a pyramidal roof. This historic courthouse is currently used for the offices of the tax commissioner and the tax assessor. In 1978, the old post office, constructed in 1896, became the primary county courthouse. It served in this function until 1995, when the newest Floyd County courthouse was completed and still today holds county offices.

Floyd County was carved from Cherokee County in 1832. It was named for General John Floyd, who commanded Georgia's troops in the War of 1812 against Great Britain.

Gilmer County

ADDRESS
1 Broad Street
Ellijay, Georgia 30540

YEAR COMPLETED
2007

ARCHITECTURAL STYLE
Modern

DESIGNER
JKH Architects

MATERIAL
Brick

CURRENT USE
Courthouse

The historic Gilmer County courthouse, with its raised porticos and four slender columns at the entrances, was originally the Hyatt Hotel, which was built in 1898. The county converted that charming adaptation of the neoclassical style into a courthouse in 1934; it was demolished in 2008. The new Gilmer County courthouse (pictured) in Ellijay is a modern facility that pays homage to the neoclassicism of the old one. The brick and glass of the main entrance is offset with a traditional four-columned portico at the end of the building's left wing.

Gilmer County was created in 1832 from Cherokee County. It is named for George Rockingham Gilmer, a state legislator, member of Congress, and two-term governor of Georgia.

Gordon County

ADDRESS
100 Wall Street
Calhoun, Georgia 30701

YEAR COMPLETED
1961

ARCHITECTURAL STYLE
Modern (Classical Revival Influences)

DESIGNER
Cunningham & Forehand

MATERIAL
Brick

CURRENT USE
Courthouse

The white marble accents on the Gordon County courthouse located in Calhoun complement the white dormers around the roof of the building. The main entrance of the courthouse is a traditional neoclassical style with a shallow portico and abbreviated white columns. Built in 1961, this courthouse replaced a Romanesque building designed by William Parkins, who also built the famous Kimball Opera House in Atlanta.

Gordon County was created in 1850. It was named after William Washington Gordon, who was the first president of the Central Railroad and Banking Company and served as a state senator.

Haralson County

ADDRESS
Old Courthouse Square
Buchanan, Georgia 30113

YEAR COMPLETED
1892

ARCHITECTURAL STYLE
Queen Anne

DESIGNER
Bruce & Morgan

MATERIAL
Brick

YEAR PLACED ON NATIONAL REGISTER
OF HISTORIC PLACES
1974

CURRENT USE
Haralson Historical Society and Library

The historic Haralson County courthouse (pictured) still stands on the square in Buchanan. Built in 1892, this courthouse has a square clock tower on one corner and a smaller round tower with a bell roof on another. The county built a new courthouse in 1972, which is a two-story building with a modern design.

Haralson County was drawn from Carroll and Polk counties in 1856. It is named for Hugh A. Haralson, a U.S. Congressman and state legislator.

Murray County

ADDRESS
121 North Third Avenue
Chatsworth, Georgia 30705

YEAR COMPLETED
1916

ARCHITECTURAL STYLE
Neoclassical Revival

DESIGNER
Alexander Blair

MATERIAL
Brick

YEAR PLACED ON NATIONAL REGISTER
OF HISTORIC PLACES
1981

CURRENT USE
Courthouse

The Murray County courthouse located in Chatsworth was built in the neoclassical style. Overlooking the scenic Cohutta Mountains, this courthouse features a large portico with a balustrade supported by the tall columns.

Murray County was created from Cherokee County in 1832. Is it named for Thomas Walton Murray, a lawyer and state legislator who served as speaker of the Georgia House of Representatives.

Paulding County

ADDRESS
11 Courthouse Square
Dallas, Georgia 30132

YEAR COMPLETED
1892

ARCHITECTURAL STYLE
Queen Anne

DESIGNER
Bruce & Morgan

MATERIAL
Brick

YEAR PLACED ON NATIONAL REGISTER
OF HISTORIC PLACES
1980

CURRENT USE
Georgia Highlands Public Library, Paulding
County and Cobb County Adult Education
Classes, Paulding Genealogy and Historical
Societies, and Paulding County Fine Arts
Association

Paulding County's courthouse in Dallas exemplifies the asymmetrical designs popular in several Georgia counties in the late nineteenth century. On the corner next to the main entrance is a large clock tower with a belfry, pyramidal roof, and stone base. A smaller octagonal tower, also with a stone base, flanks the other side of the arched entrance. Bay windows and ornate dormers add interest to the building's design.

Paulding County was designated from part of Cherokee County in 1832. It honors John Paulding, a Revolutionary War soldier who helped capture Major John André, an accomplice of Benedict Arnold.

Pickens County

ADDRESS
50 North Main Street
Jasper, Georgia 30143

YEAR COMPLETED
1949

ARCHITECTURAL STYLE
Stripped Classical

DESIGNER
Bothwell and Nash

MATERIAL
Marble over Brick

YEAR PLACED ON NATIONAL REGISTER
OF HISTORIC PLACES
2008

CURRENT USE
Courthouse

The Appalachian Mountains provide a scenic backdrop to the white marble of the Pickens County courthouse in Jasper. The marble in the structure is from local quarries, which have been an important industry to the county. Five large marble panels divide the window groupings at the main entrance of the courthouse.

Pickens County was created from Cherokee and Gilmer counties in 1853. Its name honors General Andrew Pickens of South Carolina, a Revolutionary War hero who commanded troops during the victorious Battle of Kettle Creek.

Polk County

Polk County has two courthouses in official use for county government business in Cedartown. The first courthouse (pictured), built in 1951, has a design that is modern and functional. Prominent features include the decorative square medallions of the large window panels across the front of the building and the extended bays next to the entrance. Polk Courthouse No. 2, as the county has named it, is the old city hall that was built in 1935 and renovated in 1985.

Polk County was created in 1851 from parts of Paulding and Floyd counties that were earlier part of Cherokee County. The county is named for U.S. President James K. Polk.

Walker County

ADDRESS
103 South Duke Street
LaFayette, Georgia 30728

YEAR COMPLETED
1916

ARCHITECTURAL STYLE
Beaux Arts–Renaissance Revival

DESIGNER
Charles E. Bearden

MATERIAL
Brick

YEAR PLACED ON NATIONAL REGISTER
OF HISTORIC PLACES
1980

CURRENT USE
Courthouse

The Walker County courthouse in LaFayette was built during World War I. It has six pairs of columned pilasters across the facade with rusticated features. The white trim and ornate features of the building provide a contrast to the yellow brick. The entablature across the top has a detailed relief that spans the building.

Walker County was created in 1833 from part of Murray County. It is named for Major Freeman Walker of Augusta, a lawyer and U.S. senator.

Whitfield County

ADDRESS
205 North Selvidge Street
Dalton, Georgia 30720

YEAR COMPLETED
2006

ARCHITECTURAL STYLE
Modern

DESIGNER
JKH Architects

MATERIAL
Brick

CURRENT USE
Courthouse

Whitfield County's historic courthouse located in Dalton was built in 1961. Rather than demolish the historic courthouse, the county chose to use it as the core around which a more modern facility was built in 2006. Beveled brick pilasters with glass pediments flank the door and window bays. The main entrance bay in the center has a double pediment on top.

Whitfield County was created from part of Murray County in 1851. It was named for the Reverend George Whitefield, who founded the Bethesda Orphan House in Savannah in 1740 and became one of the most influential preachers in Britain and the English colonies. The spelling of the county was changed by the state legislature in 1851 to reflect the proper pronunciation.

Northeast Georgia Mountains

Banks County

ADDRESS
106 Yonah Homer Road
Homer, Georgia 30547

YEAR COMPLETED
1863

ARCHITECTURAL STYLE
Greek Revival

DESIGNER
Samuel W. Pruitt

MATERIAL
Brick

YEAR PLACED ON NATIONAL REGISTER
OF HISTORIC PLACES
1980

CURRENT USE
Museum and Community Meeting Hall

Built during the early years of the Civil War, the historic Banks County courthouse (pictured) in Homer features four colonnettes at the entrance supported by tall brick pedestals. Exterior stairways flank the main entrance balcony on the second story. This historic courthouse was saved from demolition by the efforts of a Banks County high school student who rallied support for its restoration. The current Banks County courthouse was built in 1987 just behind the historic courthouse.

Banks County was created by the state legislature in 1858 from portions of Franklin and Habersham counties. The county is named for a circuit-riding physician, Dr. Richard Banks of Gainesville, who treated not only white settlers of the area but also Cherokee Indians when smallpox struck.

Barrow County

ADDRESS
30 North Broad Street
Winder, Georgia 30680

YEAR COMPLETED
1920

ARCHITECTURAL STYLE
Neoclassical Revival

DESIGNER
James Baldwin and R. W. Wimbish

MATERIAL
Brick

YEAR PLACED ON NATIONAL REGISTER
OF HISTORIC PLACES
1980

CURRENT USE
Administrative Offices

Barrow County's historic courthouse (pictured) built in 1920 in Winder is an example of the neoclassical style that carried into the second decade of the twentieth century. The columned portico of the main entrance has a relief in the pediment. The clock tower consists of an octagonal lantern with a small balustrade around it. The historic courthouse underwent a major renovation in 2013 and now houses the county administration. Rapid growth in the county fueled the need for a new courthouse facility, which was built in 2009.

Barrow County was created in 1914 from Gwinnett, Jackson, and Walton counties. The county is named for David Crenshaw Barrow, who served as chancellor of the University of Georgia from 1906 to 1925.

Dawson County

ADDRESS
25 Justice Way
Dawsonville, Georgia 30534

YEAR COMPLETED
2012

ARCHITECTURAL STYLE
Modern

DESIGNER
Rosser International

MATERIAL
Brick

CURRENT USE
Courthouse

Built in 2012, the Dawson County Government Center (pictured) features a modern design with an extended main entrance that includes five arches with two doors under the outer two arches and three window panels in the middle. Above the entrance are four white columned pilasters and windows with rounded pediments. Red brick pilasters line the structure above the first floor. The historic Dawson County courthouse, built in 1860, today houses the Dawson County Historic Society and the public defender's office.

Dawson County was created in 1857 from lands in Gilmer and Lumpkin counties. Dawson County and its county seat of Dawsonville bear the name of Judge William C. Dawson, who served in both houses of the state legislature as well as the U.S. Congress prior to the Civil War.

Elbert County

ADDRESS
12 South Oliver Street
Elberton, Georgia 30635

YEAR COMPLETED
1894

ARCHITECTURAL STYLE
Romanesque Revival

DESIGNER
Ruben H. Hunt

MATERIAL
Brick

YEAR PLACED ON NATIONAL REGISTER
OF HISTORIC PLACES
1980

CURRENT USE
Courthouse

In 1893, a movement began to replace the Elbert County courthouse built in 1853. The cornerstone for the courthouse that stills stands in Elberton today was laid in May 1894. This courthouse design incorporates the use of granite, which remains one of the county's key industries today. It is accentuated by a tall clock tower, steep rooflines on the corner pavilions, a high white arcade, dome, and lantern. Elbert County extensively remodeled this courthouse in 1964.

Elbert County was created in 1790 from part of Wilkes County. The county and its seat of Elberton are named for General Samuel Elbert, who commanded Continental forces in Georgia during the Revolutionary War and later served as governor from 1785 to 1786.

Forsyth County

100 Courthouse Square
Cumming, Georgia 30040

YEAR COMPLETED
1977

ARCHITECTURAL STYLE
Modern

DESIGNER
Bert T. Millard & Associates

MATERIAL
Brick

CURRENT USE
Courthouse

Located in the foothills of the North Georgia mountains in Cumming, the Forsyth County courthouse is an architectural example of the classical style. This courthouse was built to replace the 1905 historic courthouse, which burned in 1973. The tall, slender columns stretching across the portico are topped by a decorative pediment. The courthouse also features six dormers that extend across the roof over the main entrance and the golden bell dome on the clock tower.

Forsyth County was created by legislative act in 1832. It is named for John Forsyth, whose political career included serving as a U.S representative, senator, minister to Spain, governor of Georgia, and U.S. secretary of state.

Franklin County

ADDRESS
9592 Lavonia Road
Carnesville, Georgia 30521

YEAR COMPLETED
1906

ARCHITECTURAL STYLE
Neoclassical Revival

DESIGNER
Walter Chamberlain

MATERIAL
Brick

CURRENT USE
Courthouse

The combined optimism at the prospect of the arrival of new rail lines in Carnesville along with an attempt to move the county seat to Lavonia led citizens in Carnesville to contract for the building of a new Franklin County courthouse in 1906. The gray brick building is a smaller-scale neoclassical style with a portico on each of the four entrances. Two-story-high columns flank each entrance and support decoratively trimmed pediments. A dark gray dome over the clocks accentuates the white tower.

Franklin County was the first county created in Georgia after the Revolutionary War. The county is named for Benjamin Franklin, author, statesman, diplomat, philosopher, and signer of the Declaration of Independence.

Habersham County

ADDRESS
295 Llewellyn Street
Clarkesville, Georgia 30523

YEAR COMPLETED
2013

ARCHITECTURAL STYLE
Modern

DESIGNER
HOK Group Inc.

MATERIAL
Brick

CURRENT USE
Courthouse

The Habersham County courthouse (pictured) in Clarkesville was built in 2013. The courthouse entrance includes a colonnade that stretches two stories high and surrounds the main doors. A Jeffersonian dome above these columns is supported by a rounded arcade with columned pilasters. The two wings of the building extend behind the entrance in a V shape, with pavilions at each end. This courthouse replaced the previous Habersham County courthouse, which was built in 1964.

Habersham County was created in 1818 from Cherokee Indian lands. The county is named for Major Joseph Habersham, a Revolutionary War officer and later the U.S. postmaster general, serving under Presidents Washington and Adams.

Hall County

ADDRESS
225 Green Street, SE
Gainesville, Georgia 30501

YEAR COMPLETED
2002

ARCHITECTURAL STYLE
Modern

DESIGNER
Steven B. Hill and H. Lloyd Hill

MATERIAL
Brick

CURRENT USE
Courthouse

The historic Hall County courthouse, built on the square in Gainesville in 1884, was destroyed by a tornado in 1936. President Franklin D. Roosevelt expedited federal funds needed to rebuild the city, and part of those funds went toward construction of a marble courthouse in 1937. In 1975, an addition was constructed on the rear of this courthouse, making the building appear to have two entrances. In 2002, Hall County built a new courthouse (pictured) next to the historic one. This courthouse is a four-story facility with arched entrances and large arched windows on the top floor. The red brick building has a pediment over the roof at the main entrance and a number of parapets.

Hall County was created in 1818 from territory acquired through an Indian treaty. The county is named for Dr. Lyman Hall, one of three Georgia signers of the Declaration of Independence and governor of Georgia from 1783 to 1784.

Hart County

ADDRESS
165 West Franklin Street
Hartwell, Georgia 30643

YEAR COMPLETED
1971

ARCHITECTURAL STYLE
Modern

DESIGNER
James M. Hunt

MATERIAL
Brick

CURRENT USE
Courthouse

The Hart County courthouse (pictured) in Hartwell was built in 1971. The courthouse, which has a modern design, is notable for its brown brick and tiered stories. In 1987, the county dedicated on the grounds a Vietnam War memorial to honor the six men from Hart County who were killed in action. The previous Hart County courthouse, built in 1901 by J. W. Golucke, was destroyed by fire in 1967.

Hart County was created from Elbert and Franklin counties in 1853. Hart County is the only county in Georgia named for a woman, Nancy Hart of Revolutionary War fame. She gained recognition for her efforts to protect her family and community along the Broad River from British soldiers.

Jackson County

ADDRESS
5000 Jackson Parkway
Jefferson, Georgia 30529

YEAR COMPLETED
2004

ARCHITECTURAL STYLE
Classic Modern

DESIGNER
Cooper Carry Architecture

MATERIAL
Brick

CURRENT USE
Courthouse

The Jackson County courthouse (pictured) in Jefferson reflects the growth of this county in the last several decades. The facility has a modern-classical style that is similar to a number of the early-twentieth-century courthouses in Georgia. It is also dramatically different from the 1879 historic courthouse that still stands in town. The historic courthouse features an assortment of architectural designs, including Greek classicism, Italian Renaissance, and a neoclassical clock tower that was added in 1906.

Jackson County was created in 1796 from Franklin County on land formerly held by Cherokee and Creek Indians. The county is named for James Jackson, a Revolutionary War general who served in the first U.S. Congress and later as governor from 1798 to 1801.

Lumpkin County

ADDRESS
325 Riley Road
Dahlonega, Georgia 30533

YEAR COMPLETED
2010

ARCHITECTURAL STYLE
Modern

DESIGNER
Gardner Spencer Smith Tench & Jarbeau

MATERIAL
Brick

CURRENT USE
Courthouse

The Lumpkin County courthouse (pictured) in Dahlonega is in the beautiful surroundings of the mountains of North Georgia near the streams at the center of the state's antebellum gold rush. Its neoclassical characteristics blend with its modern features. The elevated portico has four tall, slender columns with capitals. A simple pediment stands high above the main entrance. Three arched frames at the entrance complement the two doorways and the center window display. The county's 1939 courthouse is now the Dahlonega Gold Museum State Historic Site, which is operated by the Georgia Department of Natural Resources. Lumpkin County is famous as the site of the country's first major gold rush, which began in 1828.

Lumpkin County was created by the state legislature in 1832 from Habersham and Hall counties. The county is named for Governor Wilson Lumpkin, who also served as a U.S. representative and senator.

Madison County

ADDRESS
101 Courthouse Square
Danielsville, Georgia 30633

YEAR COMPLETED
1901

ARCHITECTURAL STYLE
Romanesque Revival

DESIGNER
J. W. Golucke

MATERIAL
Brick

YEAR PLACED ON NATIONAL REGISTER
OF HISTORIC PLACES
1980

CURRENT USE
Chamber of Commerce, Industrial
Development and Building Authority;
County Engineer; Madison County School
Mentoring Director

Built in 1901, the Madison County historic courthouse (pictured) stands on the Danielsville town square. The Romanesque design building has an arched entrance under a large, two-tiered tower. Tall, arched windows dominate the second story. The octagonal corner pavilions, like the tower, have pyramidal roofs. In 1996, Madison County remodeled an old elementary school in Danielsville to create the Madison County government complex, where all judicial proceedings now take place.

Madison County was created by the state legislature from Franklin and Wilkes counties in 1811. The county is named for President James Madison, who was in office at that time.

Rabun County

ADDRESS
25 Courthouse Square
Clayton, Georgia 30525

YEAR COMPLETED
1967

ARCHITECTURAL STYLE
Modern

DESIGNER
John H. Harte & Associates

MATERIAL
Brick

CURRENT USE
Courthouse

The Rabun County courthouse in Clayton is ringed in the distance by the Blue Ridge Mountains in northeast Georgia. A renovation gave the courthouse a more modern style. The main entrance has a decorative gray quoining on the corners. The arch molding over the frame and the second-story windows have gray reliefs that match the quoining. This courthouse also features a clock tower that stands above the main entrance pediment.

Rabun County was created in 1819 from land ceded by the Cherokee Indians. The county is named for Governor William Rabun, who served in both the Georgia House and Senate and as governor from 1817 to 1819.

Stephens County

Tall columns support a large pediment over the portico of the main entrance of the Stephens County courthouse in Toccoa. Side entrances are in two-story pavilions with white pilasters that anchor the corners of the building. Rising behind the pediment is a large, octagonal clock tower with a green dome topped by a small lantern, which also sports a green dome.

Stephens County was created by the state legislature in 1905 from Franklin and Habersham counties. The county is named for Alexander Hamilton Stephens, a member of the U.S. Congress and later vice president of the Confederacy. Stephens also served as governor of Georgia (1882–83) and died in 1883.

Towns County

ADDRESS
48 River Street
Hiawassee, Georgia 30546

YEAR COMPLETED
1964

ARCHITECTURAL STYLE
Modern

DESIGNER
Henry M. Whitehead Jr.

MATERIAL
Brick

CURRENT USE
Courthouse

In 1964 the Towns County courthouse in Hiawassee was built in a modern style. A contemporary white arched colonnade surrounds the brown brick structure. Two-story window panes at the main entrance add interest to the building's exterior.

Towns County was created in 1856 from Rabun and Union counties. The county is named for George Washington Towns, a lawyer, legislator, and member of Congress. He served as governor of Georgia from 1847 to 1851.

Union County

ADDRESS
3 Town Square
Blairsville, Georgia 30512

YEAR COMPLETED
1899

ARCHITECTURAL STYLE
Romanesque Revival

DESIGNER
J. W. Golucke

MATERIAL
Brick

YEAR PLACED ON NATIONAL REGISTER
OF HISTORIC PLACES
1980

CURRENT USE
Union County Historical Society

The historic Union County courthouse was built in 1899 on the town square in downtown Blairsville. The low, covered arched entrance is flanked by tall bays with sharp gables. A large tower just behind the main entrance has an arched belfry beneath the four-sided clock. Arched windows, reliefs, and corner turrets also add to the building's design.

Union County was created by the state legislature in 1832 from part of Cherokee County. John Thomas, of the Union Party, the area's representative in the state legislature, said "Name it Union, for none but union-like men reside in it." Many of the early settlers were Virginians who had traveled through the Carolinas to Georgia through the mountain passages.

White County

ADDRESS
59 South Main Street
Cleveland, Georgia 30528

YEAR COMPLETED
1964

ARCHITECTURAL STYLE
Modern

DESIGNER
Jacobs and Matthews

MATERIAL
Brick

CURRENT USE
Courthouse

The White County courthouse (pictured) in Cleveland is a modern, post–World War II design with a high portico over a one-story building. This courthouse features thin rectangular columns and stone pilasters across the courthouse wings. The historic White County courthouse was built in 1859 and is still in use today as the White County Courthouse Museum.

White County was finally carved from Habersham County in 1857 after two previous attempts. The enabling act passed when State Representative David T. White of Newton County lent his support to the effort. As a result, the county was named in his honor.

Atlanta Metro

Clayton County

ADDRESS
121 South McDonough Street
Jonesboro, Georgia 30236

YEAR COMPLETED
1898

ARCHITECTURAL STYLE
Romanesque Revival

DESIGNER
J. W. Golucke

MATERIAL
Brick

CURRENT USE
County Offices

Clayton County has restored its historic courthouse in Jonesboro to its original 1898 design. The building has decorative trim, including stylish quoining on the corners. The main entrance features a large archway flanked by two smaller archways under the tall clock tower. An arched belfry, detailed relief over the clock, and spires surrounding its pyramidal roof add interest to this building's design. Clayton County's current courthouse, known as the Harold R. Banke Justice Center, opened in 2000.

Clayton County was created in 1858 by the state legislature from land carved from Fayette and Henry counties. It is named for Judge Augustin Smith Clayton, who was a U.S. Representative from Georgia and a judge for the Western Circuit.

Cobb County

ADDRESS
70 Haynes Street
Marietta, Georgia 30090

YEAR COMPLETED
2010

ARCHITECTURAL STYLE
Modern (Classical Revival Influences)

DESIGNER
Pieper O'Brien Herr Architects

MATERIAL
Brick

CURRENT USE
Courthouse

The Cobb County courthouse in Marietta covers three city blocks and has a modern design. The main entrance to the seven-story, brown brick structure is on the corner under the clock tower. Four block columns create a two-story portico that extends from the entrance along both sides of the main corner. White lintels, pilasters, and medallions also accentuate the second-story windows above these two sides of the courthouse.

Cobb County was created from Cherokee Indian territory in 1832. The county is named for Judge Thomas W. Cobb, a former U.S. senator.

Coweta County

ADDRESS
200 Court Square
Newnan, Georgia 30265

YEAR COMPLETED
1904

ARCHITECTURAL STYLE
Neoclassical Revival

DESIGNER
J. W. Golucke

MATERIAL
Brick

YEAR PLACED ON NATIONAL REGISTER
OF HISTORIC PLACES
1980

CURRENT USE
Probate Court and Welcome Center /
Visitors Bureau

The historic Coweta County courthouse (pictured) in Newnan has large four-columned porticos at the front and rear entrances and small two-columned porticos on the side entrances. The two large porticos have second-story balconies and pediments with the seal of Georgia in the medallions. The historic courthouse underwent a restoration in 2010 to return the cooper finishes on the trim and the dome of the clock tower to their 1904 state, earning the county an Excellence in Restoration award from the Georgia Trust for Historic Preservation. Coweta County built a new justice center in 2006 that is now the county's primary courthouse.

Coweta County was one of five counties created by the Treaty of Indian Springs in 1825. It is named for a Creek Indian tribe and their town, which was considered to be one of the largest centers for the Creek Nation.

DeKalb County

ADDRESS
101 East Court Square
Decatur, Georgia 30030

YEAR COMPLETED
1916

ARCHITECTURAL STYLE
Neoclassical

DESIGNER
J. W. Golucke

MATERIAL
Marble

YEAR PLACED ON NATIONAL REGISTER
OF HISTORIC PLACES
1971

CURRENT USE
DeKalb Historical Society

Built in 1916, the historic DeKalb County Courthouse (pictured) in Decatur has neoclassical features, among them white granite bricks and a grand portico. The tall, slender columns are on high pedestals and topped by capitals. The pediment has a clock insert flanked by two reliefs with finely crafted details. The county's current courthouse, built in 1967, is a modern style that reflects the growth of the county.

DeKalb County was designated in 1822 from parts of Henry, Gwinnett, and Fayette counties. Until Fulton County was established in 1853, DeKalb County encompassed the entire city of Atlanta. It is named after Baron Johann DeKalb, a German-born French officer and Revolutionary War hero.

Douglas County

ADDRESS
8700 Hospital Drive
Douglasville, Georgia 30134

YEAR COMPLETED
1998

ARCHITECTURAL STYLE
Modern

DESIGNER
Cooper Carry Inc.

MATERIAL
Brick

CURRENT USE
Courthouse

The Douglas County courthouse in Douglasville is part of a fifty-acre county complex. The main entrance of the courthouse has a portico with tall, ribbed columns. A pediment above the entrance contains the courthouse clock. The wings extending from the main entrance each have large white pilasters that rise up to a pediment. In addition, this courthouse has a central tower with four small pediments over the octagonal arcade, and above that a lantern and a dome. The previous courthouse, built in 1957, today houses a museum, the Douglas County Historical Society, and other organizations.

Douglas County was created in 1870 from Carroll and Campbell counties (the latter county no longer exists). Both the county and its seat of government, Douglasville, are named for Stephen A. Douglas, a U.S. senator from Illinois who ran against Abraham Lincoln for president in 1860.

Fayette County

ADDRESS
200 Courthouse Square
Fayetteville, Georgia 30214

YEAR COMPLETED
1825

ARCHITECTURAL STYLE
Vernacular with Second-Empire Elements

DESIGNER
Finley G. Stewart

MATERIAL
Brick

YEAR PLACED ON NATIONAL REGISTER
OF HISTORIC PLACES
1980

CURRENT USE
Fayette County Development Authority
and Mainstreet Fayetteville

The historic Fayette County courthouse (pictured) on the square in Fayetteville is the oldest courthouse still standing in Georgia. Legend has it that the Marquis de LaFayette, after whom the county and the county seat are named, was present at the time the cornerstone was set in 1825. Although the courthouse has been extensively modified with the addition of a clock tower and a third story, the original courtroom bench leading up the south entrance remains. The bench is 58 feet long and purportedly the longest such bench in the world. The current Fayette County courthouse, completed in 1985, incorporates neoclassical influences such as colonnades, a large arched entrance, and a pediment. The county also added a courthouse annex in 1992.

Fayette County, named after the French General and Revolutionary War hero Marquis de LaFayette, was created in 1821 after the Creek Indian cession of land at Indian Springs. From 1828 to 1858, four new counties were created from Fayette County land.

Fulton County

ADDRESS
160 Pryor Street, SW
Atlanta, Georgia 30303

YEAR COMPLETED
1914

ARCHITECTURAL STYLE
Beaux Arts Classicism

DESIGNER
A. Ten Eyck Brown and Morgan & Dillon

MATERIAL
Brick

YEAR PLACED ON NATIONAL REGISTER
OF HISTORIC PLACES
1980

CURRENT USE
Courthouse

The Fulton County courthouse in Atlanta was built between 1907 and 1914 and was the first courthouse in Georgia to cost over a million dollars. At the time of its construction, this courthouse had more square footage than the state capitol. The design was, according to one historian, "a modern institutional classicism" because of the combination of federal features and its massive columns, which began above the second story and reached up another five stories. Although now surrounded by taller, more modern skyscrapers, this courthouse remains prominent in downtown Atlanta.

Fulton County was created from the western half of DeKalb County in 1853 by an act of the state legislature. After the Great Depression, Fulton absorbed Milton and Campbell counties. Fulton is named for Hamilton Fulton, a railroad official who was a surveyor for the Western and Atlantic Railroad, marking the southeastern terminus that grew to become Atlanta. He was also chief engineer of the state.

Gwinnett County

ADDRESS
185 Crogan Street
Lawrenceville, Georgia 30046

YEAR COMPLETED
1885

ARCHITECTURAL STYLE
Second Empire Influences

DESIGNER
Edmund George Lind

MATERIAL
Brick

YEAR PLACED ON NATIONAL REGISTER
OF HISTORIC PLACES
1980

CURRENT USE
Gwinnett Historical Society,
Veterans Museum, Community Events,
and Private Rentals

The historic Gwinnett County courthouse (pictured) still stands on the original courthouse square in Lawrenceville; its eclectic style is the result of several additions and renovations. The building is reminiscent of a time when the county seat was a cotton mill town with several rail lines connecting the community to resources and markets across the South. In contrast, the modern Gwinnett Justice and Administration Center, built in 1988, is a large facility located south of the downtown area; its distance from the historic courthouse square reflects the phenomenal growth of the county since the 1970s.

Gwinnett County was created in 1818 from treaty lands ceded by the Creek and Cherokee Indians. It is named for Button Gwinnett, one of the three Georgia signers of the Declaration of Independence.

Henry County

ADDRESS
1 Courthouse Square
McDonough, Georgia 30253

YEAR COMPLETED
1897

ARCHITECTURAL STYLE
Romanesque Revival

DESIGNER
J. W. Golucke & Stewart

MATERIAL
Brick

YEAR PLACED ON NATIONAL REGISTER
OF HISTORIC PLACES
1980

CURRENT USE
Courthouse

The historic Henry County courthouse in McDonough has an arched main doorway extending from a double-tiered clock tower that is surrounded by spires. Ornate pediments over the tower's flanking bays add to its design interest. A large, modern annex, completed in 2000, is adjacent to the historic courthouse.

Henry County was created from Creek Indian lands in 1821. It was named for Patrick Henry, a Revolutionary War patriot and orator.

Presidential Pathways

Chattahoochee County (Cusseta–Chattahoochee County)

ADDRESS
377 Broad Street
Cusseta, Georgia 31805

YEAR COMPLETED
1976

ARCHITECTURAL STYLE
Modern

DESIGNER
Biggers, Scarbrough, Neal, Crisp & Clark

MATERIAL
Brick

YEAR PLACED ON NATIONAL REGISTER
OF HISTORIC PLACES
1980

CURRENT USE
Courthouse

The Chattahoochee County courthouse (pictured) is positioned along the rail lines that slice through the town of Cusseta. Built in 1976, the building has four square brick columns supporting a modest portico. The main entrance has arched reliefs along the facade. The historic Chattahoochee County courthouse, which still exists, was constructed of heart pine in 1854. In 1974, the county moved it from Cusseta to a nearby replicated 1850s-era community called Westville. It is one of the few wood frame courthouses still standing in the state. The city of Cusseta consolidated with Chattahoochee County in 2003.

Chattahoochee County was created from parts of Marion and Muscogee counties in 1854. The county is named for the river that Indians called Chattahoochee, meaning "rocks" that are "marked" or "painted." Cusseta, the county seat, is named for one of the principal Lower Creek Indian tribes.

Crisp County

The Crisp County courthouse in Cordele (pictured) has both modern and neoclassical features. The state legislature formed the county in 1905, and the first courthouse in Cordele followed two years later. The current courthouse was built in 1950 after the first courthouse was destroyed by fire. The raised portico has four columns that rise two stories to a rounded pediment above the main entrance. The courthouse also features faint pilasters in the red brick of the façade.

Crisp County was created from a portion of Dooly County. The county is named for Charles Frederick Crisp, a Georgia jurist and Speaker of the U.S. House of Representatives from 1891 to 1894.

Dooly County

ADDRESS
104 South Second Street
Vienna, Georgia 31092

YEAR COMPLETED
1892

ARCHITECTURAL STYLE
Romanesque Revival

DESIGNER
William H. Parkins

MATERIAL
Brick and Granite

YEAR PLACED ON NATIONAL REGISTER
OF HISTORIC PLACES
1980

CURRENT USE
Courthouse

The Dooly County courthouse in Vienna was built in 1892. The main entrance has a short, modest portico with paired square columns; a colonnade to the left leads toward the clock tower. The second story of the facade has a large, arched window topped by a pediment. The tall tower contains a louvered belfry under the clock and a belvedere on the roof. This courthouse underwent a significant renovation in 1960.

Dooly County was one of the original land lot counties that were later divided to create several other South Georgia counties. The county was designated in 1821 and named for Colonel John Dooly, a neighbor of the famed Revolutionary War patriot, Nancy Hart, for whom Hart County is named.

Harris County

ADDRESS
102 North College Street
Hamilton, Georgia 31811

YEAR COMPLETED
1908

ARCHITECTURAL STYLE
Neoclassical Revival

DESIGNER
E. C. Hosford

MATERIAL
Brick

**YEAR PLACED ON NATIONAL REGISTER
OF HISTORIC PLACES**
1980

CURRENT USE
Courthouse

The Harris County courthouse in Hamilton has six columns on a two-story portico at the former main entrance. The portico has balustrades on its second-floor balcony covered by an ornate pediment. The courthouse also features four corner pavilions.

Harris County was created in 1827 from lands formerly part of Muscogee and Troup counties. The county is named for Savannah lawyer and mayor Charles Harris.

Heard County

ADDRESS
215 East Court Square
Franklin, Georgia 30217

YEAR COMPLETED
1964

ARCHITECTURAL STYLE
Modern

DESIGNER
Tomberlin-Sheetz

MATERIAL
Brick

CURRENT USE
Courthouse

The Heard County courthouse in Franklin is a red brick facility with a low-profile roof; it resembles a number of county structures built in the post–World War II era. The previous courthouse, built in 1894, had impressively stylish features such as a clock tower and pyramidal roof. It was demolished in 1965 after this replacement was completed.

Heard County was created in 1830 from parts of Carroll, Coweta, and Troup counties. The county is named for Stephen Heard, who fought in the Revolutionary War and served as Georgia governor from 1780 to 1781.

Macon County

ADDRESS
121 South Sumter Street
Oglethorpe, Georgia 31068

YEAR COMPLETED
1894

ARCHITECTURAL STYLE
Romanesque Revival

DESIGNER
Walter Chamberlain

MATERIAL
Brick

YEAR PLACED ON NATIONAL REGISTER
OF HISTORIC PLACES
1980

CURRENT USE
Courthouse

The Macon County courthouse in Oglethorpe is an example of the Romanesque design popular in the late nineteenth century. This building has a modestly covered main entrance and pavilion compartments on the corners as well as a distinctive clock tower. The pyramidal roofs over the pavilions are adorned with red spires and dual pediments.

Macon County was created in 1837 from parts of Houston and Marion counties. The county is named for Nathaniel Macon, a North Carolina statesman and U.S. senator.

Marion County

ADDRESS
100 North Broad Street
Buena Vista, Georgia 31803

YEAR COMPLETED
1850

ARCHITECTURAL STYLE
Vernacular–Neoclassical Elements

DESIGNER
E. A. Smith

MATERIAL
Brick

YEAR PLACED ON NATIONAL REGISTER
OF HISTORIC PLACES
1980

CURRENT USE
Courthouse

Constructed in 1850, the Marion County courthouse (pictured) in Buena Vista is an example of antebellum architecture in Georgia. Originally, it was a vernacular design with little ornamentation. The classical features, including its four-columned portico and decorative pediment, date from a 1928 remodeling. Tazwell was the first county seat in Marion County, and its 1848 wood frame courthouse also still stands.

Created in 1827 from portions of Lee and Muscogee counties, Marion County is named for the Revolutionary War hero General Francis Marion, who earned the nickname the Swamp Fox.

Meriwether County

ADDRESS
100 North Court Square
Greenville, Georgia 30222

YEAR COMPLETED
1903

ARCHITECTURAL STYLE
Neoclassical Revival

DESIGNER
J. W. Golucke

MATERIAL
Brick

YEAR PLACED ON NATIONAL REGISTER
OF HISTORIC PLACES
1973

CURRENT USE
Courthouse

The Meriwether County courthouse projects a sophisticated presence on the square in downtown Greenville. All that remained of the courthouse after a 1976 fire was the brick walls. The 1980 rebuild transformed the courthouse from two floors to three. All four entrances feature porticos with high, slender limestone columns and decorative pediments. The courthouse features arched windows that wrap around the second floor. A thousand-pound clock from France on the north side chimes each hour with the musical note A. Over the lantern on the dome of the clock tower stands a statue of Lady Justice.

Meriwether County was created from Troup County in 1827. The county is named for General David Meriwether, who served in the state militia and was often called upon by the federal government to serve as an interpreter for the Creek Indians. He also was a state legislator and U.S. congressman.

Muscogee County (Columbus–Muscogee County)

ADDRESS
100 Tenth Street
Columbus, Georgia 31902

YEAR COMPLETED
1973

ARCHITECTURAL STYLE
New Formalism

DESIGNER
E. Owen Smith and Biggers, Scarbrough,
Neal, Crisp & Clark

MATERIAL
Concrete, Steel, and Glass

CURRENT USE
Courthouse

In 1971 the city of Columbus and Muscogee County officially became the first consolidated local government in Georgia. The growth that led to this extraordinary step also necessitated a larger courthouse. The old courthouse, originally built in 1838, stood immediately in front of the new multistoried building during construction but was eventually demolished.

Muscogee County was created by the state legislature in 1825 after the Creek Indians ceded large areas between the Flint and Chattahoochee Rivers in the Treaty of Indian Springs. The county is named for the original residents of the area, who were Native American.

Pike County

The Pike County courthouse in Zebulon has withstood several natural disasters over the years. The building was constructed in 1895 with a sizeable central tower, but lightning struck the tower in 1898. As part of its repair of the damage, the county built a larger tower at the front of the building, where it could be properly supported. The new tower stood over the arched entrance and was flanked by white pilasters. It also included an arcade below the clock feature and an ornate dome with decorative dormers. In 1949, however, a tornado hit the building and destroyed the top section of the restored tower. Following this incident, the county replaced the tower with an octagonal clock and a stylish bell dome visible in the photo.

Pike County was carved out of Monroe County in 1822. The county and the county seat of Zebulon honor Zebulon Pike, who led an expedition to trace the Mississippi River to its source in 1805.

Schley County

YEAR COMPLETED
1899

ARCHITECTURAL STYLE
Romanesque Revival

DESIGNER
J. W. Golucke

MATERIAL
Brick

YEAR PLACED ON NATIONAL REGISTER
OF HISTORIC PLACES
1980

CURRENT USE
Courthouse

The small community of Ellaville is home to the elegant, nineteenth-century Schley County courthouse, with its covered arched entrance and tall bay. The bays rise to sharp ornate pediments that have small, arched windows. The white window trim, banding around the building, and reliefs in the pediments accentuate the design. There is also a white tower with a clock and a pyramidal dome.

Schley County was created in 1857 from parts of Macon and Sumter counties. The county is named for William Schley, a jurist, U.S. congressman, and governor of Georgia.

Spalding County

ADDRESS
132 East Solomon Street
Griffin, Georgia 30223

YEAR COMPLETED
1985

ARCHITECTURAL STYLE
Eclectic Modern–Romanesque Influences

DESIGNER
Bibro, Spandler & Manley Architects

MATERIAL
Brick

CURRENT USE
Courthouse

The Spalding County courthouse (pictured) in Griffin was built in 1985. On one corner stands a large brick tower with a clock, and above that rises a wooden tower. The county's first courthouse, built in 1859, was originally a stylish vernacular structure with a large clock tower and steeple. The clock tower and steeple were removed in 1910, and the building was converted to a sheriff's office and jail in 1911. That building currently houses the county's Cooperative Extension and 4-H offices. Built in 1911 on the site of the current courthouse, the second courthouse was destroyed by fire in 1981.

Spalding County was created in 1851 from parts of Fayette, Henry, and Pike counties. The county is named for Thomas Spalding of Frederica, an influential farmer who cultivated Sea Island cotton and introduced the manufacture of sugar to Georgia. He also served in the state legislature and in Congress and was a member of the Constitutional Convention of 1798.

Stewart County

ADDRESS
1764 Broad Street
Lumpkin, Georgia 31815

YEAR COMPLETED
1923

ARCHITECTURAL STYLE
Neoclassical Revival

DESIGNER
T. F. Lockwood Jr.

MATERIAL
Brick

YEAR PLACED ON NATIONAL REGISTER
OF HISTORIC PLACES
1980

CURRENT USE
Courthouse

The Stewart County courthouse in Lumpkin replaced a similarly designed one that burned in 1923. When the courthouse was rebuilt, the clock tower was relocated to the front of the building, just above the main entrance. The square tower has a ribbed dome and louvered panels under the clocks on its four sides. This courthouse also has four-columned porticos at the front and rear entrances.

Created in 1830 from part of Randolph County, Stewart County is named for President Theodore Roosevelt's great-grandfather, General Daniel Stewart. Stewart was an officer in the Revolutionary War and the War of 1812.

Sumter County

ADDRESS
500 West Lamar Street
Americus, Georgia 31709

YEAR COMPLETED
2009

ARCHITECTURAL STYLE
Modern

DESIGNER
Rosser International Inc.

MATERIAL
Brick

CURRENT USE
Courthouse

Sumter County's courthouse in Americus incorporates traditional architectural style with a modern design. The arched entranceway beside the tall tower and a smaller tower on the other side of the facade reveal a Romanesque-influenced approach to this twenty-first-century building. The pyramidal roofs over these towers further reflect the blend of the traditional with new.

Sumter County was created in 1831 from lands formerly part of Lee County. The county is named for General Thomas Sumter of South Carolina, a soldier of the Revolutionary War and the French and Indian War.

Talbot County

ADDRESS
26 South Washington Avenue
Talbotton, Georgia 31827

YEAR COMPLETED
1892

ARCHITECTURAL STYLE
Queen Anne

DESIGNER
Bruce & Morgan

MATERIAL
Brick

YEAR PLACED ON NATIONAL REGISTER
OF HISTORIC PLACES
1980

CURRENT USE
Courthouse

When the historic Talbot County courthouse in Talbotton burned in 1892, the county leaders replaced it with a new facility that still serves the county today. Its most notable features include a large clock tower with a pyramidal roof, a small tower with a bell dome, and an ornate arched entrance. The arched windows, especially the tall window of the clock tower with its decorative panels, also contribute to the courthouse's design interest.

Talbot County was created in 1827 from part of Muscogee County. The county and its county seat, Talbotton, are named for Governor Matthew Talbot, a member of the convention that framed the Georgia Constitution, a long-time member of the state senate, and a former governor.

Taylor County

ADDRESS
2 North Broad Street
Butler, Georgia 31006

YEAR COMPLETED
1935

ARCHITECTURAL STYLE
Neoclassical Revival

DESIGNER
F. Roy Duncan

MATERIAL
Brick

YEAR PLACED ON NATIONAL REGISTER
OF HISTORIC PLACES
1995

CURRENT USE
Courthouse

In Butler in 1852, Taylor County built its first courthouse, which remained in use until the present courthouse (pictured) was built in 1935. This grand structure features the four-columned neoclassical portico that imparts on many Georgia courthouses a traditional southern character. All the entrances are capped by pediments, but there are pilasters instead of columns on the side entrance. An octagonal lantern tops the small central clock tower.

Taylor County was created in 1852 from parts of Macon, Marion, and Talbot counties. The county is named for Zachary Taylor, whose victory in the Battle of Buena Vista (1847) during the Mexican War positioned him for the presidency of the United States.

Troup County

ADDRESS
100 Ridley Avenue
LaGrange, Georgia 30241

YEAR COMPLETED
2005

ARCHITECTURAL STYLE
Modern

DESIGNER
Urban Design Group

MATERIAL
Brick

CURRENT USE
Courthouse and County Administration

The Troup County courthouse (pictured) in LaGrange incorporates multicolor brick in its modern design. The first two stories of the courthouse have a traditional red brick exterior with gray brick accents, while copper tiles sheathe most of the third story. The white lintels over the windows set off this color contrast. The main entrance and has a modern design featuring a colonnade. While not the original, the county's courthouse on LaFayette Square opened in 1904 and burned on November 5, 1936. The existing historic courthouse is a white marble building whose construction was subsidized by the New Deal's Works Project Administration in 1939; it currently houses the juvenile court.

Troup County was established by the state legislature in 1825 from land ceded by the Creek Indian Nation. The county is named for Governor George M. Troup, an early champion of state sovereignty who clashed with President John Adams over the issue. Atypically, the county was named for him thirty years before his death.

Upson County

ADDRESS
1 Courthouse Square
Thomaston, Georgia 30286

YEAR COMPLETED
1908

ARCHITECTURAL STYLE
Neoclassical Revival

DESIGNER
Frank P. Milburn

MATERIAL
Brick

YEAR PLACED ON NATIONAL REGISTER
OF HISTORIC PLACES
1980

CURRENT USE
Courthouse

The Upson County courthouse in Thomaston has a neoclassical design with all four entrances showcasing four-columned porticos. The columns are brown brick on high white pedestals with white capitals. These details are accentuated by the white dentils around the pediments and banding above the second floor. The central clock tower has a columned belfry and a low dome. Pilasters separate the rusticated brick pavilions from each entrance.

Upson County was created in 1824 from parts of Pike and Crawford counties. The county is named for Stephen Upson, a prominent lawyer and legislator from the antebellum period.

Webster County

(Unified Government of Webster County)

ADDRESS
6330 Hamilton Street
Preston, Georgia 31824

YEAR COMPLETED
1915

ARCHITECTURAL STYLE
Neoclassical Revival

DESIGNER
T. F. Lockwood Sr.

MATERIAL
Brick

YEAR PLACED ON NATIONAL REGISTER
OF HISTORIC PLACES
1980

CURRENT USE
Courthouse

The Webster County courthouse in Preston replaced one that burned in 1914. At the time this courthouse was built, the two-story portico, columns, and decorative pediment were familiar features on courthouses around the state by the early twentieth century. Its most unique feature is the tower atop the front pediment. Instead of a clock tower, however, the county placed a belvedere. Webster County became a consolidated government in 2008.

Webster County was created in 1853 from a portion of Stewart County. Its name honors orator and statesman Daniel Webster, whose support was critical to the passage of the Great Compromise of 1850.

Historic Heartland

Baldwin County

ADDRESS
121 North Wilkinson Street
Milledgeville, Georgia 31061

YEAR COMPLETED
1996

ARCHITECTURAL STYLE
Modern

DESIGNER
Brittain Thompson Bray Brown Inc.

MATERIAL
Brick

CURRENT USE
Courthouse

In 1996, Baldwin County built a new courthouse (pictured) in Milledgeville. The courthouse has a four-columned portico raised to the third story above the main entrance and a pediment with an arched window. A broad molded banding and clock tower add a classical look to its modern design. Milledgeville served as the state capital from 1804 through 1868, when, during Reconstruction, the Georgia legislature moved the capital to Atlanta. For a time, 1861–79, this building also served as the Baldwin County courthouse after a fire destroyed the historic courthouse that was built in 1847 and prior to the construction of the 1879 courthouse. The former state capitol and historic courthouse is now part of Georgia College and State University.

Baldwin County was created in 1803 from Creek Indian lands. It is named for Abraham Baldwin, a member of the Continental Congress and author of legislation that established the nation's first state-chartered university, the University of Georgia.

Bibb County (Macon–Bibb County)

ADDRESS
601 Mulberry Street
Macon, Georgia 31201

YEAR COMPLETED
1924

ARCHITECTURAL STYLE
Neoclassical Revival

DESIGNER
Curran R. Ellis

MATERIAL
Brick

YEAR PLACED ON NATIONAL REGISTER
OF HISTORIC PLACES
1974

CURRENT USE
Courthouse

The Bibb County courthouse in Macon has rusticated features around the first story, including the arched entrances. One of the most prominent aspects of this courthouse's design is the paired column pilasters that flank the center windows of the second and third stories at the entrances. In addition, the clock tower has a columned belfry under a cupola topped by a colorful dome. The Works Project Administration, one of the New Deal programs during the Great Depression, renovated this facility in 1940. Bibb County and the city of Macon formed a consolidated government in 2014.

Bibb County was created in 1822 from parts of Houston, Jones, Monroe, and Twiggs counties. It was named for Georgia physician Dr. William Wyatt Bibb, who served as a U.S. representative and senator from Georgia and later became Alabama's first elected governor.

Butts County

ADDRESS
25 Third Street
Jackson, Georgia 30233

YEAR COMPLETED
1898

ARCHITECTURAL STYLE
Romanesque Revival

DESIGNER
Bruce & Morgan

MATERIAL
Brick

**YEAR PLACED ON NATIONAL REGISTER
OF HISTORIC PLACES**
1980

CURRENT USE
Courthouse

The Butts County courthouse in Jackson has a main entrance with columned pilasters and an ornate crosshead that frame the archway. Other notable features include the clock tower, the arches on the belfry, reliefs, and small pediments above the clock.

Butts County was carved from Henry and Monroe counties by the state legislature in 1825 and presented to Governor George Troup as a gift. It was named for Captain Samuel Butts, a militiaman killed in the Creek Indian War of 1811–15.

OUR HEROES

IN MEMORY OF THE
CONFEDERATE SOLDIERS
OF BUTTS COUNTY
WHOSE UNDYING DEVOTION
TO DUTY AND SELF SACRIFICE
IN THEIR COUNTRY'S
SERVICE, WE CHERISH,
AND WHOSE HEROIC DEEDS
AND PATRIOTISM, WE EMBALM
IN STONE, AS THEY ARE
ENSHRINED IN OUR HEARTS.

Clarke County   (Athens–Clarke County)

ADDRESS
325 East Washington Street
Athens, Georgia 30601

YEAR COMPLETED
1914

ARCHITECTURAL STYLE
Italian Renaissance Revival and Neoclassical

DESIGNER
A. Ten Eyck Brown

MATERIAL
Brick

YEAR PLACED ON NATIONAL REGISTER
OF HISTORIC PLACES
1978

CURRENT USE
Courthouse

The Athens–Clarke County courthouse is a blend of architectural styles and is in downtown Athens. A long, narrow portico holds four columns that span almost three stories. A decorative banding wraps the courthouse above the third story. Along the roof above the entrance is a sculptured balustrade. This courthouse, with its classically influenced features, is within a short walking distance of the north campus of the University of Georgia, which has some architectural similarities. In 1991, the city of Athens and Clarke County merged to form a unified government. The old Athens city hall, a magnificent neoclassical building in its own right, then became part of the consolidated government facilities.

Clarke County received its original territory from Jackson County in 1801 as an act of the state legislature. The smallest of Georgia's 159 counties, Clarke County was named for General Elijah Clarke of Revolutionary War fame.

Crawford County

ADDRESS
100 Georgia Highway 42
Knoxville, Georgia 31050

YEAR COMPLETED
2002

ARCHITECTURAL STYLE
Modern

DESIGNER
Precision Planning

MATERIAL
Brick

CURRENT USE
Courthouse

Built in 2002, the Crawford County courthouse (pictured) in Knoxville is an elegant building faced with light-colored brick. The portico has two paired columns and pediment. Features of the square clock tower include arched windows in the lantern, a balustrade, and pediments. The historic Crawford County courthouse, built in 1832, is home to the local historical society.

Crawford County was created in 1822 from part of Houston County. Its name honors statesman William H. Crawford, who had served as a U.S. senator, minister to France, and secretary of the treasury.

Houston County

ADDRESS
201 Perry Parkway
Perry, Georgia 31069

YEAR COMPLETED
2002

ARCHITECTURAL STYLE
Modern

DESIGNER
H. D. R. and JMA Architecture Inc.

MATERIAL
Brick and Pre-cast Stone

CURRENT USE
Courthouse and County Administration

The Houston County courthouse in Perry is another showcase for blending a traditional style with a modern design. It has a neoclassically inspired main entrance with contemporary features. Rather than columns, the building is lined with white pilasters under a fashionably modern pediment. The wings of the facility have large, tinted windows, incorporating a more modern style. The previous Houston County courthouse, built in 1948, today is used for other county offices.

Houston County was created from Creek Indian land in 1821. It was named for Governor John Houstoun of the Revolutionary period. Although the spelling of the county name was changed to Houston over the years, pronunciation remains true to the original spelling.

Jasper County

ADDRESS
126 West Greene Street
Monticello, Georgia 31064

YEAR COMPLETED
1908

ARCHITECTURAL STYLE
Neoclassical Revival

DESIGNER
T. F. Lockwood Sr.

MATERIAL
Brick and Marble

YEAR PLACED ON NATIONAL
REGISTER OF HISTORIC PLACES
1980

CURRENT USE
Courthouse

The Jasper County courthouse in Monticello occupies a corner across from the town square. The white trim of the banding, pediment, and white arcade under the clock on the central tower contrast with the brown of the brick walls. The raised portico, with its four slender columns, has an arched balcony double door that matches the main double door below it.

Jasper County, created from Baldwin County in 1807, was originally named Randolph County to honor John Randolph of Virginia. However, due to Randolph's opposition to the War of 1812, the Georgia General Assembly renamed the county after Revolutionary War hero Sergeant William Jasper, who died during the siege of Savannah. By 1828 Randolph was back in Georgia's good graces and his name was given to a new county in Southwest Georgia, which still uses it today.

Jones County

ADDRESS
110 South Jefferson Street
Gray, Georgia 31032

YEAR COMPLETED
1905

ARCHITECTURAL STYLE
Romanesque Revival

DESIGNER
J. W. Golucke

MATERIAL
Brick

YEAR PLACED ON NATIONAL REGISTER
OF HISTORIC PLACES
1980

CURRENT USE
Courthouse

The Jones County courthouse in Gray is recognized by its striking clock tower, which the county restored in 2006. The courthouse has a main arched entrance on the first floor that projects from the front of a tall tower. The tower reaches high above the flanking broken pediments and includes an arcade with a balustrade. The building also has spires on the corner pavilion sections.

Jones County was created in 1807 from land acquired through the Creek Indians. It is named after James Jones, who was the principal protégé of Georgia governor James Jackson and noted adversary of the culprits behind the Yazoo land fraud.

Lamar County

ADDRESS
326 Thomaston Street
Barnesville, Georgia 30204

YEAR COMPLETED
1931

ARCHITECTURAL STYLE
Neoclassical Revival

DESIGNER
Eugene C. Wachendorff

MATERIAL
Brick

YEAR PLACED ON NATIONAL REGISTER
OF HISTORIC PLACES
1980

CURRENT USE
Courthouse

Created in 1920, Lamar County is one of the youngest Georgia counties. For the first decade of its existence, county officials used the Masonic Building for all county business. In 1931, the county built the current courthouse in Barnesville. The courthouse has an unadorned neoclassical design with a portico that has four ribbed columns supporting a pediment above the main entrance.

Formed from lands formerly in Monroe and Pike counties, the county was named for Lucius Quintus Cincinnatus Lamar, a Putnam County native. Lamar served as a U.S. senator from Mississippi, secretary of the interior, and associate justice of the U.S. Supreme Court.

Monroe County

The Monroe County courthouse on the center square in Forsyth has ornate features such as the balustrade on the connecting balcony over the main entrance, stone quoining on the corner pavilion structures, and decorative pediments on the bays flanking the main entrance. The clock tower has balustrades, turrets, and a lantern atop the dome. The previous courthouse, built in 1825, was torn down when this courthouse was opened.

Monroe County was created from Creek Indian lands in 1821. It is named for James Monroe, the fifth president of the United States.

Morgan County

ADDRESS
149 East Jefferson Street
Madison, Georgia 30650

YEAR COMPLETED
1905

ARCHITECTURAL STYLE
Neoclassical Revival

DESIGNER
J. W. Golucke

MATERIAL
Brick

YEAR PLACED ON NATIONAL REGISTER
OF HISTORIC PLACES
1974

CURRENT USE
Courthouse

Its size, shape, and location make the Morgan County courthouse one of the most noticeable structures in Madison. The V-shaped building has a large main entrance with a four-columned portico, a second-story balcony, and an arched doorway surrounded by arched windows. The main pediment holds the Georgia State Seal. Other neoclassical features include a square clock tower with a lantern on the tower dome. Each of the four sides of the tower has decorative panels lined with columned pilasters and turrets on the corners.

Morgan County was created by an act of the state legislature in 1807 from land originally in Baldwin County. It is named for Revolutionary War general Daniel Morgan, a frontiersman whose courage and abilities in battle were legendary.

Newton County

ADDRESS
1124 Clark Street
Covington, Georgia 30014

YEAR COMPLETED
1884

ARCHITECTURAL STYLE
Second Empire

DESIGNER
Bruce & Morgan

MATERIAL
Brick

YEAR PLACED ON NATIONAL REGISTER
OF HISTORIC PLACES
1980

CURRENT USE
Board of Commissioners

Built across from the town square in Covington, the Newton County courthouse has a corner tower with a large decorative clock that is capped by a dome and is surrounded by ornamental features. A lower tower sits on another corner and has a four-sided roof. This courthouse was built on the site of the previous courthouse, which was destroyed by fire on December 31, 1883.

Formed in 1821 from parts of Henry, Jasper, and Walton counties, Newton County was named for Revolutionary War hero Sergeant John Newton. Newton was said to have saved Revolutionary soldiers from execution by capturing their British guards during the Siege of Savannah in 1779.

Oconee County

ADDRESS
23 North Main Street
Watkinsville, Georgia 30677

YEAR COMPLETED
1939

ARCHITECTURAL STYLE
Stripped Classical

DESIGNER
William J. J. Chase

MATERIAL
Brick

YEAR PLACED ON NATIONAL REGISTER
OF HISTORIC PLACES
1984

CURRENT USE
Courthouse

The New Deal's Works Project Administration constructed the Oconee County courthouse in 1939 (pictured) after the old courthouse burned. Today, the courthouse sits in the historic district of downtown Watkinsville. Its white brick entrance has inlaid window panels with ribbed pilasters as a decorative framing above the main door. Red brick finishes the flanking front sides of the building, including the outside recessed wings.

Oconee County was created from part of western Clarke County in 1875 by the Georgia General Assembly. It was named for the river flowing along part of its eastern border, which comes from a Native American word meaning "spring of the hills."

Peach County

205 West Church Street
Fort Valley, Georgia 31030

YEAR COMPLETED
1936

ARCHITECTURAL STYLE
Colonial Revival

DESIGNER
Dennis & Dennis

MATERIAL
Brick

YEAR PLACED ON NATIONAL REGISTER
OF HISTORIC PLACES
1980

CURRENT USE
Courthouse

The Peach County courthouse in Fort Valley has arched front entrances under an ornate pediment with an inlaid carved peach. The courthouse also features a tall cupola on the crown of the roof and small pavilions that extend from the corners of the building.

Established in 1924, Peach County was the most recent county created in Georgia. It was carved from Houston and Macon counties. The county's name comes from the Elberta Peach. This crop also earned the county its title as "the Peach Capital of the World."

Putnam County

ADDRESS
100 South Jefferson Avenue
Eatonton, Georgia 31024

YEAR COMPLETED
1906

ARCHITECTURAL STYLE
Neoclassical Revival with Beaux Arts
Influences

DESIGNER
J. W. Golucke

MATERIAL
Brick

YEAR PLACED ON NATIONAL REGISTER
OF HISTORIC PLACES
1975

CURRENT USE
Courthouse

The present (1906) Putnam County courthouse (pictured) replaced the 1824 federal-style stuccoed brick building, which was demolished in preparation for construction of the new building. The neoclassical brick and limestone features of Golucke's design were replicated in the two large wings added in 2006. Four square brick columns on the original north and south facades support classic porticos. The four corner pavilions and the cross-hall plan of the original building remain intact. The octagonal central domed clock tower is topped by a cupola that supports a winged eagle.

Putnam County was created from part of the original Baldwin County in 1807. It is named for Revolutionary War hero General Israel Putnam, known for his contributions in the Battle of Lexington and the Battle of Breed's (Bunker) Hill.

Rockdale County

ADDRESS
922 Court Street
Conyers, Georgia 30012

YEAR COMPLETED
1939

ARCHITECTURAL STYLE
Colonial Revival

DESIGNER
William J. J. Chase

MATERIAL
Brick

YEAR PLACED ON NATIONAL REGISTER
OF HISTORIC PLACES
1988

CURRENT USE
Courthouse

The Rockdale County courthouse is in the historic district of Conyers. Built during the Great Depression, this courthouse has a Williamsburg design with a small tower on the crest of the roof.

Rockdale County was created from parts of Henry and Newton counties in 1870. Unlike most counties in Georgia, whose names honor a person, Rockdale County's name was inspired by the granite strata underlying the surface soil in the area.

Twiggs County

ADDRESS
425 Railroad Street North
Jeffersonville, Georgia 31044

YEAR COMPLETED
1904

ARCHITECTURAL STYLE
Romanesque Revival

DESIGNER
J. W. Golucke

MATERIAL
Brick

YEAR PLACED ON NATIONAL REGISTER
OF HISTORIC PLACES
1980

CURRENT USE
Courthouse

The historic Twiggs County courthouse located in Jeffersonville underwent major renovations beginning in 1979. The building's original structure was much smaller and a simpler design. Many of the building's features still remain, such as the decorative clock tower, tall pyramidal roofs, and arched entrance. The renovations involved several structural changes, such as nearly doubling the size of the pavilions on the corners and changing the brick finish from white to red.

Twiggs County was created in 1809 from land formerly in Wilkinson County. It is named for General John Twiggs, a militia leader during the Revolutionary War who helped drive the British from Georgia.

Walton County

ADDRESS
111 South Broad Street
Monroe, Georgia 30655

YEAR COMPLETED
1884

ARCHITECTURAL STYLE
Second Empire

DESIGNER
Bruce and Morgan

MATERIAL
Brick

YEAR PLACED ON NATIONAL REGISTER
OF HISTORIC PLACES
1980

CURRENT USE
Courthouse and County Offices

Built in 1884, the historic Walton County courthouse (pictured) has undergone several renovations, the most recent one in 1996. Its stick style portico at the front entrance is complemented by the balustrade on the balcony under the courtroom windows of the second story. Even the clock tower at the center has a balustrade around the top. The courthouse also has a mansard roof, ornate cornice, and Gothic dormers. The Walton County government building opened in 2004 and now serves as the primary courthouse and county administration facility.

Walton County was created in 1818 from land originally held by the Cherokee and Creek Indians. It was named for George Walton, one of the three Georgians to sign the Declaration of Independence, and later a U.S. senator and jurist.

Wilkinson County

ADDRESS
100 Bacon Street
Irwinton, Georgia 31042

YEAR COMPLETED
1924

ARCHITECTURAL STYLE
Colonial Revival

DESIGNER
Alexander Blair

MATERIAL
Brick

CURRENT USE
Courthouse

The Wilkinson County courthouse in Irwinton was built in 1924 after fire destroyed the 1870 courthouse. It has a more modest style than many courthouses built in the early twentieth century. The main entrance has columned pilasters and a broken pediment with a small circle window. The courthouse also features a central tower with louvered lantern under a dome. The county built an addition in 1974 to accommodate the offices of the tax assessor, the tax commissioner, and the board of commissioners. A second addition in 2006 added more courtroom space and judicial offices.

Wilkinson County was created in 1803 through territory acquired by cessions of the Creek Indians. It is named for Revolutionary War officer General James Wilkinson, who had been a party to the treaty that obtained the land for the county.

Classic South

Burke County

Built in 1857, the Burke County courthouse in Waynesboro is one of the older courthouses in Georgia still in use. In the original courthouse, curved stairs allowed for access to the second floor. In 1898, the front offices and clock tower were added and the stairs were removed. In 1983, the staircases were replaced.

Burke County is one of Georgia's original counties, dating back to 1777 when the first state constitution designated it from the colonial parish of St. George. It was later divided to form Screven, Jefferson, Richmond, and Jenkins counties. Its name honors Edmund Burke, a member of the British Parliament who supported the colonies' interests.

Columbia County

ADDRESS
640 Ronald Reagan Drive
Evans, Georgia 30809

YEAR COMPLETED
2001

ARCHITECTURAL STYLE
Modern

DESIGNER
Rosser International Inc.

MATERIAL
Brick

CURRENT USE
Courthouse

The Columbia County Justice Center (pictured) in Evans is a modern building with neoclassical influences. Six columns sit on the portico, and three sets of double doors at the main entrance feature ornate pediments. There also is a cupola on the roof ridge. The complex forms a horseshoe that partially encloses a courtyard at the main entrance. The historic Columbia County courthouse, built in 1856, still stands in the unincorporated community of Appling.

Columbia County was formed in 1790 through an act of the state legislature by taking part of the northern area of Richmond County. It was created out of necessity at the behest of its white backcountry settlers as a more convenient area to hold court than Augusta. It was named for explorer Christopher Columbus.

Emanuel County

ADDRESS
125 South Main Street
Swainsboro, Georgia 30401

YEAR COMPLETED
2002

ARCHITECTURAL STYLE
Modern

DESIGNER
James W. Buckley & Associates

MATERIAL
Brick

CURRENT USE
Courthouse

The Emanuel courthouse in Swainsboro is a one-story facility. Its narrow portico has five arched entranceways. A stucco banding wraps around the building just above the entranceways and windows of the wings. The decorative quoining on the corners adds further detail. The previous courthouse, built in 1940, was torn down, and a park was created on the historic courthouse square.

Emanuel County was created in 1812 by combining parts of Bulloch and Montgomery counties. It was named for David Emanuel, a Revolutionary War veteran who was governor of Georgia in 1801. Five counties were later formed from land contributed by Emanuel County.

Glascock County

ADDRESS
62 East Main Street
Gibson, Georgia 30810

YEAR COMPLETED
1919

ARCHITECTURAL STYLE
Neoclassical Influences

DESIGNER
J. W. McMillian & Son

MATERIAL
Brick

YEAR PLACED ON NATIONAL REGISTER
OF HISTORIC PLACES
1980

CURRENT USE
Courthouse

The Glascock County courthouse (pictured) in Gibson is a rich red, with an ornamental frame around the main door. Steeply pitched roofs alternate with flat bays around the building, giving it additional dimensional character. Glascock County also has one of five antebellum wood frame courthouses still standing in Georgia. This courthouse was moved from its original location and is now a private residence.

Glascock County was created in 1857 from part of Warren County. It is named for General Thomas Glascock, who earned his rank as general in the War of 1812 and in the Seminole War. He later served as Speaker of the Georgia House and as a member of Congress.

Greene County

ADDRESS
113 North Main Street
Greensboro, Georgia 30642

YEAR COMPLETED
1849

ARCHITECTURAL STYLE
Greek Revival

DESIGNER
David Demarest & Atharates Atkinson

MATERIAL
Brick

YEAR PLACED ON NATIONAL REGISTER
OF HISTORIC PLACES
1980

CURRENT USE
Courthouse

The Greene County courthouse in Greensboro is an excellent example of a Greek Revival building from antebellum Georgia. The entrance to the courthouse features four columns under a simple pediment.

In 1786, Greene County was created to become Georgia's eleventh county. Both the county and its seat of government, Greensboro, were named after a respected general of the Revolutionary War, Nathanael Greene.

Hancock County

ADDRESS
12630 Broad Street
Sparta, Georgia 31087

YEAR COMPLETED
1883

ARCHITECTURAL STYLE
Second Empire

DESIGNER
Parkins and Bruce

MATERIAL
Brick

YEAR PLACED ON NATIONAL REGISTER
OF HISTORIC PLACES
1974

CURRENT USE
Courthouse

The Hancock County courthouse in Sparta occupies a prominent position on the town square. The courthouse has a double-tiered clock tower, an enlarged second story, and a squat front porch at the entrance.

Hancock County received its territory from Greene and Washington counties in 1793. Its name honors John Hancock, who presided over the Continental Congress and whose signature caps the list of signers of the Declaration of Independence.

Jefferson County

202 East Broad Street
Louisville, Georgia 30434

YEAR COMPLETED
1904

ARCHITECTURAL STYLE
Neoclassical Revival

DESIGNER
W. F. Denney

MATERIAL
Brick

YEAR PLACED ON NATIONAL
REGISTER OF HISTORIC PLACES
1980

CURRENT USE
Courthouse

From 1796 to 1806, Georgia's third state capital was in Louisville in Jefferson County. The county's last three courthouses were built on the same spot over the years. The first of these courthouses was the old capitol building. The present courthouse, built in 1904 (pictured), still has the foundation from the 1848 courthouse underneath it. This courthouse is exquisitely designed with a neoclassical style that includes four slender, high columns and a balustrade on the portico. The main pediment is beautifully adorned, and the clock tower is one of its most elegant features.

Jefferson County was created from parts of Burke and Warren counties in 1796 and named for Thomas Jefferson, primary author of the Declaration of Independence and in 1796, elected vice president of the United States.

Jenkins County

ADDRESS
611 East Winthrope Avenue
Millen, Georgia 30442

YEAR COMPLETED
1910

ARCHITECTURAL STYLE
Neoclassical Revival

DESIGNER
L. F. Goodrich

MATERIAL
Brick

YEAR PLACED ON NATIONAL REGISTER
OF HISTORIC PLACES
1980

CURRENT USE
Courthouse and County Administrative
Offices

Atop the Jenkins County courthouse in Millen stands a sculpture of Blind Justice resting on the dome of the clock tower. This is the second courthouse in the county's history, replacing one built two years earlier that burned. The new courthouse is nearly identical to the first. This neoclassical structure features an unusual clock tower, six columns that are three stories high, and a second-floor balcony on the portico.

Jenkins County was created by an act of the state legislature in 1905 by land obtained from Bulloch, Burke, Emanuel, and Screven counties. It is named for judge and Reconstruction-era governor Charles J. Jenkins.

Johnson County

2557 East Elm Street
Wrightsville, Georgia 31096

ARCHITECTURAL STYLE
Neoclassical Revival

YEAR COMPLETED
1895

DESIGNER
J. W. Golucke & Stewart

MATERIAL
Brick

YEAR PLACED ON NATIONAL REGISTER
OF HISTORIC PLACES
1980

CURRENT USE
Courthouse

The Johnson County courthouse in Wrightsville is on the town square. The two-story brick building has pavilions on the corners. These sections of the building are massive relative to the center of the courthouse and overshadow its small entrances. The original courthouse clock tower was removed in 1938 due to insufficient structural support and was replaced with the current neoclassical clock tower.

Johnson County was created in 1858 from parts of Emanuel, Laurens, and Washington counties. It was named for Hershel V. Johnson, who served as governor of Georgia between 1853 and 1857. He also served as a superior court judge from 1873 to 1880 and has the distinction of being the only judge in Georgia history to sit on the bench in the superior court of a county named for him.

Lincoln County

ADDRESS
210 Humphrey Street
Lincolnton, Georgia 30817

YEAR COMPLETED
1915

ARCHITECTURAL STYLE
Neoclassical Revival

DESIGNER
G. Lloyd Preacher

MATERIAL
Brick

YEAR PLACED ON NATIONAL REGISTER
OF HISTORIC PLACES
1980

CURRENT USE
Courthouse

The Lincoln County courthouse in Lincolnton has a neoclassical design. Four ribbed columns ascend more than two stories above the portico to undergird a decorative pediment. The main entrance has a balustrade on the courthouse balcony. A small lantern sits atop the clock tower's metal dome, which matches the metal roof.

Lincoln County was created from part of Wilkes County in 1796. It is named for Major General Benjamin Lincoln, who played a key role in the defeat of the British at Yorktown.

McDuffie County

ADDRESS
210 Railroad Street
Thomson, Georgia 30824

YEAR COMPLETED
2011

ARCHITECTURAL STYLE
Modern

DESIGNER
Bryant Associates

MATERIAL
Brick

CURRENT USE
Courthouse and Offices for City and
County Administration

The Thomson-McDuffie Government Center built in 2011 (pictured) is an example of how an architectural design can utilize traditional styles and make them modern. In addition to a contemporary portico with four columns, the building is divided into a series of extended and recessive bays. Pilasters and white lintels over the windows decorate these bays. In addition, the building features a series of narrow white banding that surrounds the upper stories of the facility. The historic McDuffie County courthouse was built in 1872 and expanded in 1934.

McDuffie County was created in 1870 by an act of the Georgia General Assembly from land provided by Columbia and Warren counties. It is named for George McDuffie, a native Georgian lawyer and statesman who became a governor and U.S. senator for South Carolina.

Oglethorpe County

ADDRESS
111 West Main Street
Lexington, Georgia 30648

YEAR COMPLETED
1887

ARCHITECTURAL STYLE
Romanesque Revival

DESIGNER
Lorenzo B. Wheeler, William H. Parkins,
and Hannibal I. Kimball

MATERIAL
Brick

YEAR PLACED ON NATIONAL REGISTER
OF HISTORIC PLACES
1977

CURRENT USE
Courthouse

The Oglethorpe County courthouse in Lexington is among the most unusual courthouses in the state. A tall clock tower rises in the center over the main entrance. This tower holds a Seth Thomas clock purportedly weighing as much as a ton. Rounded tourelles sit on granite pedestals and frame the corners of the tower. The red brick building and the tower have white granite arches over the entranceways and window, as well as pronounced granite banding around the structure.

Oglethorpe County, named for Georgia's founder James Oglethorpe, was carved from Wilkes County in 1793.

Richmond County (Augusta–Richmond County)

ADDRESS
735 James Brown Boulevard
Augusta, Georgia 30901

YEAR COMPLETED
2011

ARCHITECTURAL STYLE
Modern

DESIGNER
Turner & Associates

MATERIAL
Brick

CURRENT USE
Courthouse and Associated Court-Related
Offices

The Augusta Judicial Center and John H. Ruffin Jr. Courthouse, built in 2011, spans 180,000 square feet, has a 35-foot-high ceiling in the lobby, and houses eighteen courtrooms. The courthouse also has an architectural design that is modern with a retro-classical appeal. This building has a number of interesting features. The two-story convex structure that flows from the main entrance is lined with a series of tall panels of windows for both floors. The main entrance also connects to the four-story section of the courthouse and has a white, four-columned portico. Near the center of the roof is a large, white, square colonnade that mimics the white portico.

Richmond County was created in 1777 as one of Georgia's original counties. The county was named for Charles Lenox, duke of Richmond, who was sympathetic to the cause of the American Revolution.

Taliaferro County

ADDRESS
113 Monument Street
Crawfordville, Georgia 30631

YEAR COMPLETED
1902

ARCHITECTURAL STYLE
High Victorian Eclectic

DESIGNER
Lewis F. Goodrich

MATERIAL
Brick

YEAR PLACED ON NATIONAL REGISTER
OF HISTORIC PLACES
1980

CURRENT USE
Courthouse

The Taliaferro County courthouse was built in Crawfordville in 1902. Two entrances have portico roofs with balustrades under the courtroom window and a dormer on the roof. The dormer pediment on the main entrance has a detailed relief of the scales of justice. At one corner rise a tall, octagonal clock tower with a dome. The smaller tower has a handsome bell tower.

Taliaferro County was created in 1825 from Greene, Hancock, Oglethorpe, Warren, and Wilkes counties. It was named for Benjamin Taliaferro, a colonel during the American Revolution who later served as a Georgia legislator and a superior court judge.

Warren County

ADDRESS
521 Main Street
Warrenton, Georgia 30828

YEAR COMPLETED
1909

ARCHITECTURAL STYLE
Neoclassical Revival

DESIGNER
Brittain Thompson Bray Brown Inc.

MATERIAL
Brick

YEAR PLACED ON NATIONAL REGISTER
OF HISTORIC PLACES
1980

CURRENT USE
Courthouse

The Warren County courthouse in Warrenton is a blend of old and new. The classical features from the early twentieth century remained intact after a major renovation in 2000 that doubled the size of the building. The large portico has two-story columns at the main entrance, white pilasters, and white quoining on the corners. The courthouse also has a tower in the center of the mansard roof.

Warren County was created in 1793 from Burke, Columbia, Washington, and Wilkes counties. It and its county seat, Warrenton, were named after Joseph Warren, a colonial physician and Revolutionary War soldier.

Washington County

ADDRESS
132 West Haynes Street
Sandersville, Georgia 31082

YEAR COMPLETED
1869

ARCHITECTURAL STYLE
High Victorian Eclectic (Second-Empire
Elements)

DESIGNER
Greene Bentley and J. W. Renfoe

MATERIAL
Brick

YEAR PLACED ON NATIONAL REGISTER
OF HISTORIC PLACES
1980

CURRENT USE
Courthouse

The Washington County courthouse is on the square in downtown Sandersville. First built in 1869, it replaced the courthouse that was burned during the Civil War. By 1896, the county began to prosper and support grew for a new courthouse. Quickly, however, rural opposition emerged. Consequently, a compromise was reached to remodel the historic courthouse. Among the building's features are a tall corner clock tower with small pediments, dormers with reliefs, and double banding above the first floor.

Washington County was established on February 25, 1784, and was named for General George Washington.

Wilkes County

ADDRESS
23 Court Street
Washington, Georgia 30673

YEAR COMPLETED
1904

ARCHITECTURAL STYLE
Richardsonian Romanesque

DESIGNER
Frank P. Milburn

MATERIAL
Brick

YEAR PLACED ON NATIONAL REGISTER
OF HISTORIC PLACES
1980

CURRENT USE
Courthouse

Excitement over the coming of the railroad to Washington in Wilkes County generated support for a new courthouse. In 1904, Wilkes County built a brown-brick courthouse with an exceptional design. The low arch of the main entrance is tightly placed between a round pavilion on one corner and its tall clock tower. A fire in 1958 destroyed the courthouse room and tower. While the building was repaired, it was not restored to its pre-1958 appearance until 1989, when a rear addition was also built.

Wilkes County was created in 1777 as Georgia's first county. It is named for John Wilkes, a member of British Parliament who opposed many of the British policies that eventually led to the American Revolution. The county seat, Washington, is thought to be the first town in the United States to be named for George Washington.

Plantation Trace

Baker County

ADDRESS
100 Main Street
Newton, Georgia 39870

YEAR COMPLETED
1906

ARCHITECTURAL STYLE
Romanesque Revival

DESIGNER
J. W. Golucke

MATERIAL
Brick

YEAR PLACED ON NATIONAL REGISTER
OF HISTORIC PLACES
1980

CURRENT USE
Library

The historic Baker County courthouse (pictured) in Newton was built in 1906. The tall clock tower hovers directly over the main entrance and has a high-pitched pyramidal roof. The corners of the pavilions are set with turrets and bays flank the tower. Since the construction of this courthouse in 1906, it was rebuilt twice after major floods in 1925 and 1994 destroyed much of the building, with the waters rising six and seventeen feet, respectively. The historic courthouse is now being used as a library. In 2000, the courthouse was moved into a vacant school building that was built in 1933.

Baker County was created in 1825 from territory that was once part of Early County. The county is named for Colonel John Baker, a Revolutionary War hero in the Battle of Kings Mountain, South Carolina. He also served in the 1775 Provincial Congress in Savannah.

Berrien County

ADDRESS
201 North Davis Street
Nashville, Georgia 31639

YEAR COMPLETED
2008

ARCHITECTURAL STYLE
Modern

DESIGNER
Glenn Gregory & Associates

MATERIAL
Brick

CURRENT USE
Courthouse and County Administration

Built in 2008, the Berrien County courthouse (pictured) in Nashville is a modern building that has notable classical features. The four slender columns sitting at the front of the tall portico support a pediment with a blue fanlight. The style of the historic Berrien County courthouse in Nashville is typical of the late nineteenth century and features rusticated reliefs, pyramidal roofs with spires, and a clock tower. The historic courthouse grounds are also the site of the first in a series of memorial statues, The Spirit of the American Doughboy, a tribute to World War I veterans that soon appeared in other locations across the nation.

Berrien County was created in 1856 from parts of Coffee, Irwin, and Lowndes counties. The county is named for John Macpherson Berrien, a U.S. senator from Georgia and President Andrew Jackson's attorney general.

Brooks County

ADDRESS
1 Screven Street
Quitman, Georgia 31643

YEAR COMPLETED
1864

ARCHITECTURAL STYLE
Italian Renaissance Revival

DESIGNER
John Wind

MATERIAL
Brick

YEAR PLACED ON NATIONAL REGISTER
OF HISTORIC PLACES
1980

CURRENT USE
Courthouse

The white brick and gray-trimmed Brooks County courthouse in Quitman was finished in 1864 and extensively renovated in 1892. The main entrance contains a double-arched entrance with decorative reliefs. Above these arches are two windows with a pediment over each. At the top of the main entrance is a single pediment with a fanlight. The courthouse also uses rustication and quoins on the corners and has a colorful clock tower. The bricks used to build this courthouse came from local Georgia clay.

Brooks County was created in 1858 from portions of Thomas and Lowndes counties. The county is named for Preston Brooks, a defender of states' rights and a South Carolina member of Congress prior to the Civil War.

Calhoun County

ADDRESS
31 Court Street
Morgan, Georgia 39866

YEAR COMPLETED
1935

ARCHITECTURAL STYLE
Colonial Revival

DESIGNER
T. F. Lockwood Jr.

MATERIAL
Brick

YEAR PLACED ON NATIONAL REGISTER
OF HISTORIC PLACES
1954

CURRENT USE
Courthouse

The Calhoun County courthouse in Morgan is an example of the continuing popularity of classical influences on Georgia courthouse architecture. The four columns on the portico support a pediment with a circular medallion. A white banding stretches around the building just above the second story. On the crest of the roof is a simple white octagonal tower that has arched louver panels.

Land once part of Baker and Early counties now comprises Calhoun County. Created in 1854, the county is named for Senator John C. Calhoun of South Carolina, who also served as vice president under John Quincy Adams and Andrew Jackson, and additionally as secretary of war and state.

Clay County

ADDRESS
210 South Washington Street
Fort Gaines, Georgia 39851

YEAR COMPLETED
1873

ARCHITECTURAL STYLE
Vernacular (Greek Revival Influences)

DESIGNER
Unknown

MATERIAL
Brick

YEAR PLACED ON NATIONAL REGISTER
OF HISTORIC PLACES
1980

CURRENT USE
Courthouse

The Clay County courthouse in Fort Gaines has a style that was common in small, rural counties in the nineteenth century. Its square, wooden columns at the main entrance frame a second-floor balcony. It also has simple but stylish pilasters and a pyramidal roof.

Clay County was created from parts of Early and Randolph counties in 1854. One of the state's most western counties, it was named for U.S. Senator Henry Clay of Kentucky, the most important voice nationally for western and frontier interests.

Clinch County

ADDRESS
25 Court Square
Homerville, Georgia 31634

YEAR COMPLETED
1896

ARCHITECTURAL STYLE
Victorian and Neoclassical

DESIGNER
T. J. Darling

MATERIAL
Brick

YEAR PLACED ON NATIONAL REGISTER
OF HISTORIC PLACES
1980

CURRENT USE
Courthouse

In 1860, Clinch County moved its courthouse from the community of Magnolia to a location that would be closer to a stop along the railroad. This stop was on property owned by Dr. John Homer Mattox, who gave the rail line a right-of-way and donated the land for the courthouse. As a result, Homerville was created. Built in 1896, the courthouse features a vernacular design with square posts at the main entrance that support a tall portico with a handsome second floor balcony. During the Great Depression, the Works Project Administration of the New Deal remodeled this courthouse, adding the front columns and the second-floor balcony.

Clinch County was created in 1850 from land that had been part of Lowndes and Ware counties. It was named for Duncan Lamont Clinch, a veteran of the War of 1812 and a Georgia congressman.

Colquitt County

ADDRESS
9 North Main Street
Moultrie, Georgia 31768

YEAR COMPLETED
1902

ARCHITECTURAL STYLE
Neoclassical Revival

DESIGNER
Andrew J. Bryan and Co.

MATERIAL
Marble

YEAR PLACED ON NATIONAL REGISTER
OF HISTORIC PLACES
1980

CURRENT USE
Courthouse

The Colquitt County courthouse in Moultrie has undergone major renovations since its construction in 1902. A 1952 renovation painted over the red brick and added another story to the building. A 2001 renovation retained the new story and painted brick but otherwise restored much of the building to its original design. This courthouse has neoclassical entrances on all sides and a prominent octagonal clock tower at the center. The tower features a balustrade, small columns and pediment of the clock, and a gray dome.

Colquitt County was created from Lowndes and Thomas counties in 1856. The county is named for the Reverend Walter T. Colquitt, who served as a U.S. senator and a local judge as well as a Methodist minister.

Cook County

ADDRESS
1200 South Hutchinson Avenue
Adel, Georgia 31620

YEAR COMPLETED
1939

ARCHITECTURAL STYLE
Stripped Classical

DESIGNER
William J. J. Close

MATERIAL
Brick

YEAR PLACED ON NATIONAL REGISTER
OF HISTORIC PLACES
1995

CURRENT USE
Courthouse

The Cook County courthouse in Adel was built during the Great Depression by the New Deal's Works Project Administration. This courthouse, constructed using light-colored brick, has reliefs over the windows and door of the first floor. There are also four decoratively detailed pilasters that line the front and a rounded, stone pediment over the main entrance.

Cook County was created from land in Berrien County in 1918. The county is named for General Philip Cook, who fought in both the Seminole War and the Civil War, then served in Congress. He also served as Georgia secretary of state and was a member of the commission that oversaw construction of the state capitol in Atlanta.

Decatur County

112 West Water Street
Bainbridge, Georgia 39817

YEAR COMPLETED
1902

ARCHITECTURAL STYLE
Neoclassical Revival

DESIGNER
Alexander Blair

MATERIAL
Brick

YEAR PLACED ON NATIONAL REGISTER
OF HISTORIC PLACES
1980

CURRENT USE
Courthouse

Adjacent to the public park on the town square, the Decatur County courthouse in Bainbridge was built in 1902. The architecture is a blend of architectural styles that make the building unique. In addition to a tall campanile with clock, a low corner tower has windows with decorative lintels and reliefs. Both towers also have balustrades. A traditional portico stands at the main entrance with its four columns and large pediment.

Decatur County was created in 1823 from portions of Early County. The county is named for Commodore Stephen Decatur, a naval leader in the War of 1812 and the Barbary War of 1815.

Dougherty County

ADDRESS
225 Pine Avenue
Albany, Georgia 31701

YEAR COMPLETED
1968

ARCHITECTURAL STYLE
Modern

DESIGNER
Harry A. MacEwen and Edward V. Jones

MATERIAL
Masonry

CURRENT USE
Courthouse

The Dougherty County courthouse in Albany has distinctive features, such as its U-shaped design. Five archways allow access to the modern-styled portico. Double-ribbed pilasters line the wings of the building, which project from the main entrance. Built in 1903, the historic Dougherty County courthouse was devastated by a tornado in 1940, rebuilt, and finally burned in 1966.

Dougherty County was created in 1853 from part of Baker County. The county is named for Judge Charles Dougherty of Athens, an advocate of states' rights.

Early County

ADDRESS
111 Court Square
Blakely, Georgia 39823

YEAR COMPLETED
1905

ARCHITECTURAL STYLE
Neoclassical Revival

DESIGNER
Morgan & Dillon

MATERIAL
Brick

YEAR PLACED ON NATIONAL REGISTER
OF HISTORIC PLACES
1980

CURRENT USE
Courthouse

Once one of the largest counties in South Georgia, Early County built its courthouse in Blakely in 1905. The porticos at the main entrances have four columns that are partially beveled. A large ornate pediment stands over each entrance with a circle window as an insert. Two side entrances have similar porticos with only two columns. At the center is a tower that rests on an octagonal pedestal, with unusual hooded clocks, and a dome. All of the corners and pilasters on the courthouse are rusticated. The current courthouse was built in 1905 and was rehabitated in 1992.

Early County was designated in 1818 directly from Creek Indian land. The county is named for Peter Early, who served as governor of Georgia from 1813 to 1815. He was also a member of Congress and judge of the Ocmulgee Circuit.

Echols County

(Echols County Consolidated Government)

ADDRESS
110 Highway 94 East
Statenville, Georgia 31648

YEAR COMPLETED
1956

ARCHITECTURAL STYLE
Modern

DESIGNER
W. Conner Thomson

MATERIAL
Brick

CURRENT USE
Courthouse

Built in 1956, the Echols County courthouse is the third courthouse for the county. True to its design as a mid-twentieth-century, modern structure, it features clean lines and lacks adornment. The courthouse is in the unincorporated community of Statenville, which consists solely of the courthouse square.

Echols County was created from Clinch and Lowndes counties in 1858. The county is named for Robert M. Echols, who commanded troops in the Mexican War after serving as a member of the Georgia General Assembly for over twenty years. Echols County became a consolidated government in 2008.

Grady County

ADDRESS
250 North Broad Street
Cairo, Georgia 39828

YEAR COMPLETED
1985

ARCHITECTURAL STYLE
Classic Revival

DESIGNER
Jinright, Ryan and Lynn Architects

MATERIAL
Brick

CURRENT USE
Courthouse

There have only been two courthouses in Grady County since its creation in 1905. The first, a Renaissance Revival style with a stout clock tower, burned in 1980. The more classical building, built in 1985 (pictured), is absent a clock tower but features white pilasters and dormers.

Grady County was created from parts of Decatur and Thomas counties. The county is named for Henry W. Grady, editor of the *Atlanta Constitution* during the Reconstruction Period and an advocate of the "New South."

Lanier County

ADDRESS
56 West Main Street
Lakeland, Georgia 31635

YEAR COMPLETED
1973

ARCHITECTURAL STYLE
Modern

DESIGNER
Thomas Sanders

MATERIAL
Brick

CURRENT USE
Courthouse

Two courthouses have served Lanier County since its creation in 1920. The current courthouse (pictured), built in 1973 in Lakeland, has a very modest design. Accounts conflict about how long the county's first courthouse was in use as a courthouse. Some sources state that it opened in 1921, a year after the legislature established the county. Another source, however, indicates that the county used the upper floor of a merchant store for county business until 1942.

Lanier County was created from parts of Berrien, Clinch, and Lowndes counties. The county is named for Sidney Lanier, a Georgia poet, novelist, and composer.

Lee County

ADDRESS
100 Leslie Highway
Leesburg, Georgia 31763

YEAR COMPLETED
1918

ARCHITECTURAL STYLE
Neoclassical Revival

DESIGNER
J. J. Baldwin

MATERIAL
Brick

YEAR PLACED ON NATIONAL REGISTER OF HISTORIC PLACES
1980

CURRENT USE
Courthouse

The Lee County courthouse in Leesburg is a neoclassical structure from the second decade of the twentieth century. The brown brick, white and brown trim, and the copper dome on the clock tower lend interest to the building. In addition to the four-columned portico and ornate pediment, the corners have rusticated quoining.

Lee County was created by the Georgia General Assembly in 1825 from lands the Creek Indians ceded by treaty.

Lowndes County

108 East Central Avenue
Valdosta, Georgia 31601

YEAR COMPLETED
1905

ARCHITECTURAL STYLE
Neoclassical Revival

DESIGNER
Frank P. Milburn

MATERIAL
Brick

YEAR PLACED ON NATIONAL REGISTER
OF HISTORIC PLACES
1980

CURRENT USE
Courthouse

The Lowndes County courthouse in Valdosta was built in 1905. This courthouse marks the seventh courthouse in the county's history, as a result of changes to the location of the county seat, fires, and construction of newer facilities. This courthouse has a raised four-columned portico, a white balustrade around the roof, and windows hooded with pediments. The two-tiered central tower has its own columns, balustrades, and spires. The decorative gray domes capping the four corner pavilions match the gray dome over the tower.

Lowndes County was created from Irwin County in 1825. The county name honors William Jones Lowndes, whose father, Rawlins Lowndes, was a Revolutionary War hero from South Carolina.

Miller County

ADDRESS
155 North First Street
Colquitt, Georgia 39837

YEAR COMPLETED
1977

ARCHITECTURAL STYLE
Modern

DESIGNER
Tomberlin & Associates

MATERIAL
Brick

CURRENT USE
Courthouse

Today's Miller County courthouse in Colquitt was built in 1977. Four decorative brick archways at the main entrance simulate classical columns. The 1906 historic Miller County courthouse was destroyed by fire in 1974.

Miller County was created from Baker and Early counties in 1856. The county is named for Judge Andrew J. Miller, who served in the state senate and later became president of the Medical College of Georgia (now Georgia Health Sciences University).

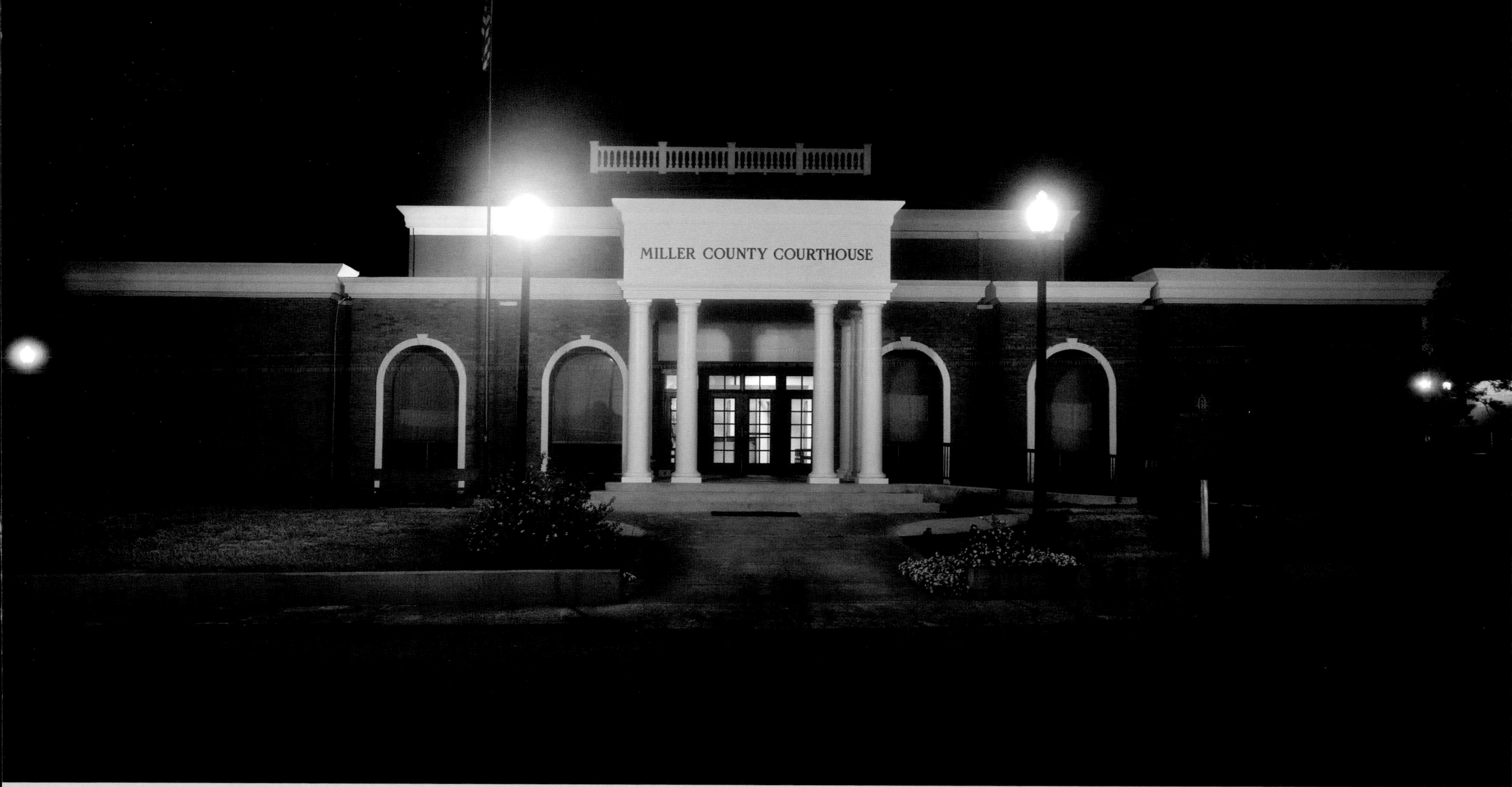
MILLER COUNTY COURTHOUSE

Mitchell County

ADDRESS
11 West Broad
Camilla, Georgia 31730

YEAR COMPLETED
1936

ARCHITECTURAL STYLE
Stripped Classical

DESIGNER
William J. J. Chase

MATERIAL
Marble

YEAR PLACED ON NATIONAL REGISTER
OF HISTORIC PLACES
1981

CURRENT USE
Courthouse

The Mitchell County courthouse in Camilla is constructed of polished Georgia marble. Built by the New Deal's Works Project Administration during the Great Depression, the courthouse has a clock above the main entrance between etchings of two American eagles. This courthouse also has decorative window panels with ornate pilasters.

Mitchell County was created from Baker County in 1857. Historians cite two possible sources for the county name. It is either named for General David B. Mitchell, who twice served as governor of Georgia, or General Henry Mitchell, who served in the Revolutionary War as well as a state senator from this county.

Quitman County (Georgetown–Quitman County)

ADDRESS
111 Main Street
Georgetown, Georgia 39854

YEAR COMPLETED
1939

ARCHITECTURAL STYLE
Stripped Classical (Colonial Revival Elements)

DESIGNER
T. F. Lockwood Jr.

MATERIAL
Brick

YEAR PLACED ON NATIONAL REGISTER
OF HISTORIC PLACES
1995

CURRENT USE
Courthouse

Quitman County's first courthouse was a two-story wood frame structure in Georgetown. This building served the county until it burned in 1921. Subsequently, county officials met in a rented commercial warehouse until federal money from the New Deal became available to build a new courthouse (pictured) in 1939. Its features include white ornate pilasters that simulate columns at the main entrance and decorative windows in the brick bays flanking the front door.

Quitman County was created from land in Randolph and Stewart counties in 1858. The county is named for General John A. Quitman, a Mexican War leader and governor of Mississippi.

Randolph County

ADDRESS
51 Court Street
Cuthbert, Georgia 39840

YEAR COMPLETED
1886

ARCHITECTURAL STYLE
Queen Anne

DESIGNER
Kimball, Wheeler & Parkins

MATERIAL
Brick

YEAR PLACED ON NATIONAL REGISTER
OF HISTORIC PLACES
1975

CURRENT USE
Randolph County Welcome Center

Built in 1886, the historic Randolph County courthouse (pictured) now serves as the Randolph County Welcome Center. This courthouse has a large corner clock tower with an ornate banding around the high dome. The courtroom window over the main entrance has a balcony under it and an arched relief over it. The courthouse also has a scrolling design on the front pediment, a dormer over the back entrance and pyramidal roofs.

Randolph County was created in 1828 from Lee County and is named for Virginia congressman John Randolph.

Seminole County

ADDRESS
200 South Knox Avenue
Donalsonville, Georgia 39845

YEAR COMPLETED
1922

ARCHITECTURAL STYLE
Neoclassical Revival and Beaux Arts

DESIGNER
William J. J. Chase

MATERIAL
Brick

YEAR PLACED ON NATIONAL REGISTER
OF HISTORIC PLACES
1980

CURRENT USE
Courthouse and Local Government

The Seminole County courthouse in Donalsonville is known as the Two Palms Courthouse because of the tropical trees on either side of its wide entrance walk. Located on the square in Donalsonville, this courthouse has four white columns at the main entrance as well as white window trim and entablature. Ornate medallions on the facade flank the entablature as well as the balustrade on the roof.

Seminole County was created in 1920 from parts of Decatur and Early counties. The county name pays tribute to the Seminole Indians who inhabited the area and who were part of the Muscogee tribe of the Lower Creeks.

Terrell County

ADDRESS
235 East Lee Street
Dawson, Georgia 39842

YEAR COMPLETED
1892

ARCHITECTURAL STYLE
High Victorian Eclectic

DESIGNER
William H. Parkins

MATERIAL
Brick

YEAR PLACED ON NATIONAL REGISTER
OF HISTORIC PLACES
1980

CURRENT USE
Courthouse

The Terrell County courthouse in Dawson has a stunning design. The two towers have long turrets on their outside corners. The tall clock tower has small turrets surrounding the pyramidal roof, while the small tower at the far corner features an arcade below its lantern and steeple. Stone arches at the main entrance and a low pediment over another entrance are among the striking features of this ornate courthouse. The stepped parapet over the main entrance is also noteworthy.

Terrell County was created from Randolph and Lee counties in 1856. The county is named for physician and statesman Dr. William Terrell of Sparta, who had served in both the state legislature and in Congress.

Thomas County

ADDRESS
225 North Broad Street
Thomasville, Georgia 31792

YEAR COMPLETED
1858

ARCHITECTURAL STYLE
Greek Revival–Victorian

DESIGNER
John Wind

MATERIAL
Brick

YEAR PLACED ON NATIONAL REGISTER
OF HISTORIC PLACES
1970

CURRENT USE
Board of Commissioners, Tax Assessor,
and Tax Commissioner

The Thomas County courthouse in Thomasville was built in 1858 by Brewer Brothers of Thomas County for $14,999. This courthouse has undergone a number of renovations over the years, including one completed in 2013. Today the courthouse features a four-columned portico with a small columned belfry on top, an enclosed portico, three arched entrances on the first floor, and an octagonal clock tower with a dome. In 1937, an annex was added to the courthouse to house the administrative offices and the board of commissioners. Thomas County built a new judicial center in 2009.

Thomas County was created from Decatur and Irwin counties in 1825. The name of the county as well as the county seat of Thomasville is named after General Jett Thomas, a hero in the War of 1812 and later a builder of the state capitol in Milledgeville.

Tift County

ADDRESS
237 East Second Street
Tifton, Georgia 31794

YEAR COMPLETED
1913

ARCHITECTURAL STYLE
Beaux Arts Classicism

DESIGNER
W. A. Edwards

MATERIAL
Brick

YEAR PLACED ON NATIONAL REGISTER
OF HISTORIC PLACES
1980

CURRENT USE
Courthouse

Built in 1913, the Tift County courthouse in Tifton is a handsome brown-brick building with a four-columned portico featuring an ornate relief at the top. Rusticated pilasters, topped with parapets at the roof, flank the main entrance.

Tift County was created in 1905 from portions of Berrien, Irwin, and Worth counties. The founder of the county was Henry Harding Tift; however, since Georgia law did not allow for counties to be named after a living person, it was named for Nelson Tift, his uncle and a civic and political leader in the Albany area. The Georgia General Assembly, at the request of the Tift County Board of Commissioners, renamed the county for Henry Harding Tift through the passage of legislation in 2013.

Turner County

ADDRESS
219 East College Avenue
Ashburn, Georgia 31714

YEAR COMPLETED
1907

ARCHITECTURAL STYLE
Eclectic Neoclassical Revival

DESIGNER
Alexander Blair and P .E. Dennis

MATERIAL
Brick

YEAR PLACED ON NATIONAL REGISTER
OF HISTORIC PLACES
1980

CURRENT USE
Courthouse

The Turner County courthouse in Ashburn has a narrow, two-story portico with paired columns at the entrance with a finely decorated pediment. The tall campanile supports an elegant clock tower with a lantern and an octagonal dome. The brown quoining on all corners and the white banding above the second floor are representative of the detailed attention given to this design.

Turner County was created in 1905 from portions of Dooly, Irwin, Wilcox, Worth, and Dooly counties. The county is named for Confederate Captain Henry Gray Turner, a veteran of Gettysburg, who also served as a member of Congress and the state legislature as well as a Georgia Supreme Court justice.

Worth County

ADDRESS
201 North Main Street
Sylvester, Georgia 31791

YEAR COMPLETED
1905

ARCHITECTURAL STYLE
Neoclassical Revival

DESIGNER
J. W. Golucke

MATERIAL
Brick

YEAR PLACED ON NATIONAL REGISTER
OF HISTORIC PLACES
1980

CURRENT USE
Courthouse

Located in Southwest Georgia, Worth County's neoclassical courthouse in Sylvester has four-columned and two-columned porticos on its entrances, with detailed pediments that stretch two stories. At the main entrance is a medallion of the seal of Georgia in the pediment. An ornate banding that matches the style of the pediments surrounds the courthouse above the second floor. The dark brown clock dome and lantern dome contrast with the building's brown brick. The courthouse suffered a fire in 1982 and required a major renovation that replicated much of the structure as it was constructed in 1906.

Worth County was created in 1853 from portions of Dooly and Irwin counties. The county is named for Major General William J. Worth, a commander who gained fame in the Mexican War.

Magnolia Midlands

Appling County

ADDRESS
36 South Main Street
Baxley, Georgia 31513

YEAR COMPLETED
1907–1908

ARCHITECTURAL STYLE
Neoclassical Revival

DESIGNER
H. L. Lewman

MATERIAL
Limestone

YEAR PLACED ON NATIONAL REGISTER
OF HISTORIC PLACES
1980

CURRENT USE
Courthouse

The Appling County courthouse in Baxley has classical porticos, two-story columns, pediments, and limestone walls. The octagonal clock tower has a bell dome under the lantern. The rusticated brick around the porticos are accented with smooth corners.

Appling County was created by legislative act in 1818 from treaty lands ceded by the Creek Indians. It is named for Colonel Daniel Appling, who was regarded as Georgia's most prominent soldier of the War of 1812.

Atkinson County

The Atkinson County courthouse in Pearson has several classical features. The four-columned portico has doubled pilasters to separate the main entrance from the wings. Medallions decorate the ends of the entablature of the facade. The clock tower has a louvered lantern and a dome.

Atkinson County was created in 1917 and contains lands previously part of Clinch and Coffee counties. It is named for William Y. Atkinson, Speaker of the Georgia House of Representatives and two-term governor from 1894 to 1898 who condemned lynching and the convict lease system.

Bacon County

YEAR COMPLETED
1919

ARCHITECTURAL STYLE
Neoclassical Revival

DESIGNER
J. J. Baldwin

MATERIAL
Brick

YEAR PLACED ON NATIONAL REGISTER
OF HISTORIC PLACES
1980

CURRENT USE
Courthouse

The Bacon County courthouse in Alma has a neoclassical revival style. The columned portico is capped with a large, pediment that has a checkered medallion. A brick pedestal supports a clock tower crowned with a beveled dome. On the center bay are three large windows with arches above the first floor. Finally, the corners of the pavilions are rusticated, which adds further detail to the design.

Bacon County was created in 1914 from portions of Appling, Pierce, and Ware counties. The county is named for Augustus O. Bacon, a U.S. senator who served four terms and was president pro tempore of the senate in 1912.

Ben Hill County

ADDRESS
402 A East Pine Street
Fitzgerald, Georgia 31750

YEAR COMPLETED
1909

ARCHITECTURAL STYLE
Southern Colonial Revival

DESIGNER
H. H. Huggins

MATERIAL
Brick

YEAR PLACED ON NATIONAL REGISTER
OF HISTORIC PLACES
1980

CURRENT USE
Courthouse

The Ben Hill courthouse in Fitzgerald was built in 1909. The columned porticos with pediments at all four entrances are made of brown brick. There are also balconies under the courtroom windows on the second story. A white balustrade wraps the roof.

Ben Hill County was created from parts of Irwin and Wilcox counties in 1906. The county is named for staunch Reconstruction leader Benjamin Harvey Hill, who served in both the U.S. and the Confederate Congress.

Bleckley County

Located in Cochran, Bleckley County's courthouse has a large portico with four large columns extending above the second floor. The pediment resting on these columns has an inlaid relief. The main entrance has a decorative concrete door frame and hood. The courthouse also has white, rusticated quoining on its corners; the clock tower on the dome is accented by dark panels.

Bleckley County was created from Pulaski County through constitutional amendment in 1912. It was named for Georgia Supreme Chief Justice Logan E. Bleckley, whose written opinions often circulated nationally.

Bulloch County

ADDRESS
2 North Main Street
Statesboro, Georgia 30458

YEAR COMPLETED
1894

ARCHITECTURAL STYLE
Queen Anne (Neoclassical Revival Elements)

DESIGNER
Bruce & Morgan

MATERIAL
Brick

YEAR PLACED ON NATIONAL REGISTER
OF HISTORIC PLACES
1980

CURRENT USE
Courthouse

Built in 1894, the Bulloch County courthouse in Statesboro acquired some neoclassical features after its extensive remodeling in 1914. The remodeling added columned porticos and entrances with column pilasters flanking the doors and pediments overhead. A clock tower sits just behind the left corner of the facade. This tower features reliefs under the clock and broken pediments over it.

Bulloch County was created in 1796 from treaty lands acquired from the Creek Indians. This county is named for Georgia's first chief executive and commander in chief, Archibald Bulloch, the great-great grandfather of President Theodore Roosevelt.

Candler County

ADDRESS
35 SW Broad Street
Metter, Georgia 30439

YEAR COMPLETED
1921

ARCHITECTURAL STYLE
Neoclassical Revival

DESIGNER
J. J. Baldwin

MATERIAL
Brick

YEAR PLACED ON NATIONAL REGISTER
OF HISTORIC PLACES
1980

CURRENT USE
Courthouse

The Candler County courthouse in Metter is a brown-brick building that includes a four-columned portico and pediment enhanced with a circular glass medallion. A thick, white banding runs below the first story and above the second-story windows. This courthouse also has rusticated quoining on all of the corners and a square clock tower with a brown dome.

Candler County was created in 1914 from parts of Bulloch, Emanuel, and Tattnall counties. The county is named for Governor Allen D. Candler, who served from 1898 to 1902. Candler is credited with researching and preserving many of the state's colonial, revolutionary, and Confederate records.

Coffee County

ADDRESS
101 South Peterson Street
Douglas, Georgia 31533

YEAR COMPLETED
1940

ARCHITECTURAL STYLE
Stripped Classical

DESIGNER
William J. J. Chase

MATERIAL
Brick and Limestone

YEAR PLACED ON NATIONAL REGISTER
OF HISTORIC PLACES
1993

CURRENT USE
Courthouse

Coffee County constructed its current courthouse in Douglas in 1940 during the Great Depression. The two columns on either side of the small doorway are identical at the front and rear entrances. The rusticated brick of the lower facade contrasts with the smooth brick of the upper-story facades. The front of the courthouse has a pavilion on each corner.

Coffee County was created in 1854 from parts of Clinch, Irwin, Telfair, and Ware counties. The county is named for General John Coffee, who served in both houses of the Georgia State Legislature as well as in the U.S. Congress. He also fought in the region's Indian wars.

Dodge County

ADDRESS
5016 Courthouse Square
Eastman, Georgia 31023

YEAR COMPLETED
1908

ARCHITECTURAL STYLE
Neoclassical Revival

DESIGNER
E. C. Hosford

MATERIAL
Brick

YEAR PLACED ON NATIONAL
REGISTER OF HISTORIC PLACES
1980

CURRENT USE
Courthouse

Today the Dodge County courthouse in Eastman bears little resemblance to the building that was constructed in 1908. In 1939, a fire swept through the building and destroyed much of the interior and the two main entrances. One of the notable casualties of the fire was the elegant clock tower with its stylish bell dome. Today the main entrances have porticos with paired columns supporting pediments. The second-story windows of the portico have balconies with balustrades.

Created in 1870 from parts of Montgomery, Pulaski, and Telfair counties, Dodge County is named for William E. Dodge, a New York lumberman who owned vast timber acreage in Georgia and is credited with persuading Congress to remove taxation from timber. Dodge also built the county's first courthouse as a gift in 1870.

Evans County

ADDRESS
123 West Main Street
Claxton, Georgia 30417

YEAR COMPLETED
1923

ARCHITECTURAL STYLE
Neoclassical Revival

DESIGNER
J. J. Baldwin

MATERIAL
Brick

YEAR PLACED ON NATIONAL REGISTER
OF HISTORIC PLACES
1980

CURRENT USE
Courthouse

The Evans County courthouse in Claxton is the county's first and only courthouse. This neoclassical-style building features a large portico with four tall, slender columns that lift up a pediment. The central clock tower has a louvered arcade with a gold dome resting above the clocks.

Evans County was created in 1914 from parts of Tattnall and Bulloch counties. The county is named for General Clement A. Evans, a Georgia native who participated in every major battle of the Confederate Army of Northern Virginia.

Irwin County

ADDRESS
301 South Irwin Avenue
Ocilla, Georgia 31774

YEAR COMPLETED
1910

ARCHITECTURAL STYLE
Neoclassical Revival

DESIGNER
Falls City Construction (H. L. Lewman)

MATERIAL
Brick

YEAR PLACED ON NATIONAL REGISTER
OF HISTORIC PLACES
1980

CURRENT USE
Courthouse

The Irwin County courthouse in Ocilla features four entrances that have raised porticos with four slender columns ascending three stories to elegant pediments. The dark brown color on its central clock tower is a contrast to the building's light brown brick. The construction of this courthouse became necessary in 1907 when the county seat moved from Irwinville to Ocilla.

Irwin County was one of seven counties created by the state legislature in 1818 from land acquired from the Creek Indians in the 1814 Treaty of Fort Jackson. The county is named for Governor Jared Irwin, who served two terms (1796–98 and 1807–9). A colonel during the Revolutionary War, Irwin also served as brigadier general in the state militia and several terms as a state legislator.

Jeff Davis County

ADDRESS
14 Jeff Davis Street
Hazlehurst, Georgia 31539

YEAR COMPLETED
1907

ARCHITECTURAL STYLE
Neoclassical Revival

DESIGNER
W. Chamberlain

MATERIAL
Concrete Block

YEAR PLACED ON NATIONAL REGISTER
OF HISTORIC PLACES
1980

CURRENT USE
Courthouse

Built in 1907, the Jeff Davis County courthouse in Hazlehurst was the first one in Georgia constructed of concrete. This courthouse underwent renovations and additions in 1995. Arched entrances, broad, white banding, and pyramidal roofs decorate the building. It also has round pavilions on the corners and a louvered clock tower with a dome.

Jeff Davis County was created from parts of Appling and Coffee counties in 1905. The county is named for Jefferson Davis, president of the Confederate States of America.

Laurens County

ADDRESS
101 North Jefferson Street
Dublin, Georgia 31040

YEAR COMPLETED
1962

ARCHITECTURAL STYLE
Modern Federal with Abbreviated Classical

DESIGNER
Cunningham and Forehand

MATERIAL
Brick

CURRENT USE
Courthouse

Laurens County has had four courthouses throughout the county's history. The first courthouse was a temporary facility built in 1811 for $36. Today's courthouse (pictured) in Dublin was built in 1962 for just under a million dollars. This courthouse has four neoclassical columns that stand on a simple portico supporting a marble pediment. Behind the portico is a two-story, rectangular structure with a flat roof.

Laurens County was created by the state legislature in 1807 from part of Wilkinson County. The county's name commemorates Colonel John Laurens of South Carolina. An aide to General George Washington and the son of a president of the Continental Congress, Laurens was killed in 1783 during the American Revolution.

Long County

ADDRESS
459 South McDonald Street
Ludowici, Georgia 31316

YEAR COMPLETED
1926

ARCHITECTURAL STYLE
Neoclassical Revival

DESIGNER
G. M. Harrington

MATERIAL
Brick

YEAR PLACED ON NATIONAL REGISTER
OF HISTORIC PLACES
1980

CURRENT USE
Courthouse

The Long County courthouse in Ludowici has a neoclassical design. The courthouse front portico has four pillars supporting a traditional pediment. Built in 1926, this courthouse lacks the clock tower that accompanies many neoclassical courthouses. With the official standardization of time across the United States in 1918, courthouse clocks lost their functional importance to become more of a stylistic choice.

Long County was established from land in Liberty County in 1920. The county name honors Dr. Crawford W. Long, a physician who discovered ether as anesthesia for surgery.

Montgomery County

ADDRESS
400 Railroad Avenue
Mount Vernon, Georgia 30445

YEAR COMPLETED
1907

ARCHITECTURAL STYLE
Neoclassical

DESIGNER
Alexander Blair

MATERIAL
Brick

YEAR PLACED ON NATIONAL REGISTER
OF HISTORIC PLACES
1980

CURRENT USE
Courthouse

The Montgomery County courthouse on the town square in Mount Vernon was built in the neoclassical style. It has four columns on the portico, a Greek triglyph above the entrance, and a clock tower. The building also features pavilions on the corners with low pyramidal roofs.

Montgomery County was created from Washington County in 1793. With the Revolutionary War still fresh in their minds, founders named this county for Continental Army Brigadier General Richard Montgomery, who was killed at the siege of Quebec.

Pulaski County

ADDRESS
141 Commerce Street
Hawkinsville, Georgia 31036

YEAR COMPLETED
1874

ARCHITECTURAL STYLE
Vernacular and Neoclassical Revival

DESIGNER
Unknown

MATERIAL
Brick

YEAR PLACED ON NATIONAL REGISTER
OF HISTORIC PLACES
1980

CURRENT USE
Courthouse

Located in Hawkinsville, the Pulaski County courthouse was built in 1874 in a vernacular style. In 1885, the county added the white, octagonal central tower next to the clock panels. In 1897, the courthouse was remodeled to include a neoclassical portico with an ornate pediment supported by four columns.

Pulaski County was created from Laurens County in 1808. The county is named for Casimir Pulaski, one of Georgia's most notable military heroes during the Revolutionary War. A Polish officer, Pulaski was killed during the 1779 Siege of Savannah.

Screven County

ADDRESS
ADDRESS
216 Mims Road
Sylvania, Georgia 30467

YEAR COMPLETED
1964

ARCHITECTURAL STYLE
Modern

DESIGNER
Sewell & Associates

MATERIAL
Brick

CURRENT USE
Courthouse

The Screven County courthouse in Sylvania is the county's eighth judicial building since the county's creation in 1793. Built in 1964, the current courthouse is a one-story, modern red brick structure with brown banding under the eaves of the green roof. The main entrance sits at the juncture of the two wings that form into a right angle.

Screven County was created from parts of Burke and Effingham counties. This land was part of the colonial parishes of St. Phillip and St. Matthew. The county is named for Revolutionary War General James Screven of Midway, who was mortally wounded in a 1778 battle near Midway Church.

Tattnall County

108 West Brazell Street
Reidsville, Georgia 30453

YEAR COMPLETED
1902

ARCHITECTURAL STYLE
Second Empire

DESIGNER
J. W. Golucke

MATERIAL
Brick

CURRENT USE
Board of Commissioners and
Administrative Offices

The Tattnall County courthouse in Reidsville was constructed in 1902 and most recently renovated in 2009. Its ornate arched entrances match the arched windows that line the first floor. The second story outside the courtroom has a window balcony with a balustrade. Across this balcony are four columns that support a rounded pediment. This courthouse had a highly pitched mansard roof with decorative dormers and a clock tower, which were removed during a 1964 renovation.

Tattnall County was created in 1801 from a portion of Montgomery County and named for Governor Josiah Tattnall Sr., who signed the legislation creating the county just one month after taking office. Tattnall was educated at Eaton College in England, served in the Continental Army during the Revolutionary War, and rose to the rank of brigadier general in the Georgia militia. He served as governor from 1801 to 1802.

Telfair County

ADDRESS
19 East Oak Street
McRae, Georgia 31055

YEAR COMPLETED
1934

ARCHITECTURAL STYLE
Colonial Revival

DESIGNER
Dennis & Dennis

MATERIAL
Brick

YEAR PLACED ON NATIONAL REGISTER
OF HISTORIC PLACES
1995

CURRENT USE
Courthouse

Built in 1934, the Telfair County courthouse in McRae has four pairs of white pilasters that simulate columns around the courtroom windows over the front entrance on the second floor. Three archways mark the entrance to the main doors. The building also has pavilions at the corners. The side entrance has a pediment over the door and arched windows across the first floor that are connected to a white decorative banding through the windows on the first story of the building.

Telfair County was created in 1807 from part of Wilkinson County. The county is named for Governor Edward Telfair, who served three terms in this office in the late 1700s. Born in Scotland, Telfair sailed to the English colonies in 1758, where he later established himself as a successful merchant in Savannah. He championed the colonies' complaints against King George III and served as a Georgia member of the Continental Congress.

Toombs County

ADDRESS
100 Courthouse Square
Lyons, Georgia 30436

YEAR COMPLETED
1964

ARCHITECTURAL STYLE
Modern

DESIGNER
W. P. Thompson Jr.

MATERIAL
Brick

CURRENT USE
Courthouse

The Toombs County courthouse in Lyons is a mid-twentieth-century modern building. The main entrance is lined with white panels of floor-length windows that stretch to the adjoining wings. The left wing is the only two-story section of the courthouse. The historic 1919 courthouse was demolished in 1964.

Toombs County was created in 1905 from portions of Tattnall, Montgomery, and Emanuel counties. The county is named for General Robert Toombs, a former U.S. representative and senator who went on to serve the Confederacy as secretary of state and brigadier general and, later, as the leading force behind the new state constitution of 1877.

Treutlen County

The Treutlen County courthouse in Soperton is another example of the charming neoclassical structure that appeared in the early twentieth century. Its two-story portico has four columns that support a pediment at the main entrance. A central tower has a large octagonal lantern that has an ornate setting for the clock and dome. The courthouse also features white trim, banding, and tower.

Treutlen County was created from Emanuel and Montgomery counties in 1918. The county is named for John Adam Treutlen, who served in the Provincial Congress of 1775, helped draft the first state constitution of 1777, and subsequently became Georgia's first governor.

Wayne County

ADDRESS
174 North Brunswick Street
Jesup, Georgia 31546

YEAR COMPLETED
1903

ARCHITECTURAL STYLE
Romanesque Revival

DESIGNER
S. A. Baker

MATERIAL
Brick

YEAR PLACED ON NATIONAL REGISTER
OF HISTORIC PLACES
1980

CURRENT USE
Courthouse

The Wayne County courthouse in downtown Jesup has a tall clock tower over the main entrance with a louvered belfry and a pyramidal roof. The courthouse also has pediments over the side entrances and arched windows around the second story.

Wayne County was created in 1803 on land acquired from the Creek Indians as part of the 1802 Treaty of Fort Wilkinson. The county is named for General Anthony Wayne, a Revolutionary War leader from Pennsylvania who conducted daring exploits against the British in several southern campaigns.

Wheeler County

ADDRESS
16 West Pearl Street
Alamo, Georgia 30411

YEAR COMPLETED
1917

ARCHITECTURAL STYLE
Neoclassical Revival

DESIGNER
Ed C. Hosford and Frank P. Milburn

MATERIAL
Brick

YEAR PLACED ON NATIONAL REGISTER
OF HISTORIC PLACES
1980

CURRENT USE
Courthouse

Built in 1917, the Wheeler County courthouse in Alamo has a traditional, two-story neoclassical design. The courthouse features four-columned porticos at all of its entrances. The county renovated the courthouse in 1961.

Wheeler County was created from Montgomery County in 1912. The county is named for General Joseph Wheeler, who served in the Confederate cavalry during the Civil War. President William McKinley appointed him major general during the Spanish-American War (1898), with Theodore Roosevelt's Rough Riders serving under his command.

Wilcox County

ADDRESS
103 North Broad Street
Abbeville, Georgia 31001

YEAR COMPLETED
1903

ARCHITECTURAL STYLE
Neoclassical Revival

DESIGNER
Frank P. Milburn

MATERIAL
Brick

YEAR PLACED ON NATIONAL REGISTER
OF HISTORIC PLACES
1980

CURRENT USE
Courthouse

The Wilcox County courthouse in Abbeville is a brown-brick building with four-columned porticos that stretch three stories high. Detailed pediments hang over its entrances. The building also has rusticated brick quoining on the corner and a clock tower with a lantern.

Wilcox County was created in 1857 with land from Dooly, Irwin, and Pulaski counties. Historians disagree about the origin of Wilcox County's name. Georgia archives show the county is named after General Mark Wilcox, a soldier in the Indian Wars who later served in the Georgia General Assembly and was one of the founders of the U.S. Supreme Court. Others believe it was named for his father, Captain John Wilcox.

The Coast

Brantley County

ADDRESS
234 Brantley Street
Nahunta, Georgia 31553

YEAR COMPLETED
1930

ARCHITECTURAL STYLE
Modern

DESIGNER
T. J. Darling

MATERIAL
Brick

YEAR PLACED ON NATIONAL REGISTER
OF HISTORIC PLACES
1980

CURRENT USE
Courthouse

The Brantley County courthouse is in Nahunta. Above the arched door of the main entrance is a small balcony with its own arched French door. A small tower stands over the main entrance and a clock is inserted into the pediment.

Brantley County is made up of parts of Charlton, Pierce, and Wayne counties. It was created in 1920 by the Georgia General Assembly after a citizens committee asked the state to provide them with a more localized government for their area. The county name comes from the Brantley family, although it is unclear whether it is named for Benjamin Daniel Brantley, a merchant, or for his son, William Gordon Brantley, who served in both houses of the state legislature and in the U.S. House of Representatives.

Bryan County

ADDRESS
151 South Courthouse Street
Pembroke, Georgia 31321

YEAR COMPLETED
1938

ARCHITECTURAL STYLE
Neoclassical Revival

DESIGNER
Walter P. Marshall

MATERIAL
Brick

YEAR PLACED ON NATIONAL REGISTER
OF HISTORIC PLACES
1995

CURRENT USE
Courthouse

The Bryan County courthouse in Pembroke has a classical-inspired four-columned portico with a pediment that contains a clock. The main entrance is taller than the wings to accommodate the large courtroom on the second floor. Two pavilions with their pyramidal roofs straddle the main entrance.

Bryan County was created from Chatham County by an act of the General Assembly in 1793. The county was named for Jonathan Bryan, a colonial settler and a key figure in Georgia's move toward independence during the Revolutionary War.

Camden County

ADDRESS
210 East Fourth Street
Woodbine, Georgia 31569

YEAR COMPLETED
2004

ARCHITECTURAL STYLE
Modern

DESIGNER
Buckley & Associates

MATERIAL
Brick

CURRENT USE
Courthouse

The Camden County courthouse (pictured) in Woodbine has a broad portico with four columns that stretch across the main entrance. A pediment stretches over the arched courthouse windows of the second story. The other windows on the second story also have pediments. Brick pilasters separate the building's sections. The historic courthouse, built in 1928, also still stands in Woodbine.

Camden County was created by the Georgia Constitution in 1777 and is the state's eighth original county. It was named for Charles Pratt, Earl of Camden, Chief Justice and Lord Chancellor of England. Pratt was a strong supporter of the colonies prior to the Revolutionary War.

Charlton County

ADDRESS
1520 Third Street
Folkston, Georgia 31537

YEAR COMPLETED
1928

ARCHITECTURAL STYLE
Neoclassical Revival (Georgian Revival
Influences)

DESIGNER
Roy A. Benjamin

MATERIAL
Brick

YEAR PLACED ON NATIONAL REGISTER
OF HISTORIC PLACES
1980

CURRENT USE
Courthouse

Located at the end of Main Street in Folkston, the Charlton County courthouse has a neoclassical design. Some of the building's features include two paired columns on the portico, a decorative relief clock in the pediment, and a balustrade across the roof's facade. It also has quoining on the corners. A renovation of the building has brought back much of its original characteristics. This courthouse replaced the 1902 building that burned in 1928.

Charlton County was designated in 1854 from parts of Camden and Ware counties. It was named for Senator Robert M. Charlton, who served as a jurist, U.S. senator, and mayor of Savannah.

Chatham County

ADDRESS
124 Bull Street
Savannah, Georgia 31401

YEAR COMPLETED
1889

ARCHITECTURAL STYLE
Romanesque Revival

DESIGNER
William G. Preston

MATERIAL
Yellow Brick

YEAR PLACED ON NATIONAL REGISTER
OF HISTORIC PLACES
1966

CURRENT USE
County Administrative and Legal Offices

The historic Chatham County courthouse (pictured), on Bull Street in Savannah, is an eclectic building with several unique features. Constructed of yellow brick, the building has tourelles on the low tower and a balcony balustrade at the top. The clock tower has a hooded pyramidal roof. Today the historic courthouse houses the county's administrative and legal offices; judicial proceedings are held in the courthouse that was built in 1978.

Consisting of lands from Christ Church and St. Phillip parishes, Chatham was the fifth county to be designated in Georgia in 1777. It is named for English prime minister William Pitt the Elder, Earl of Chatham.

Effingham County

ADDRESS
901 North Pine Street
Springfield, Georgia 31329

YEAR COMPLETED
1908

ARCHITECTURAL STYLE
Neoclassical Revival

DESIGNER
Hyman W. Whitcover

MATERIAL
Brick

YEAR PLACED ON NATIONAL REGISTER
OF HISTORIC PLACES
1980

CURRENT USE
County Offices

The Effingham County courthouse (pictured) in Springfield was built in 1908 and renovated in 2010. Three columns stand on both sides of the extended portico at its main entrance. The entrance has a rounded gray pediment with an engraved medallion.

Effingham County is the fourth of the state's original eight counties. It was created from the parishes of St. Matthew and St. Philip. The county was named for Thomas Howard, the third earl of Effingham, who was a supporter of the colonies leading up to the Revolutionary War.

Glynn County

ADDRESS
701 H Street
Brunswick, Georgia 31520

YEAR COMPLETED
1991

ARCHITECTURAL STYLE
Renaissance and Neoclassical Revival

DESIGNER
Hansen, Lind, Meyer Inc. and W. S. Ledbetter

MATERIAL
Brick

CURRENT USE
Courthouse

Located in Brunswick, Glynn County's courthouse illustrates how features of a historic courthouse can be incorporated into the design of a new facility. The historic Glynn County courthouse, built in 1907, still stands among the mossy oak trees, palm trees, and azaleas on the old courthouse square in Brunswick. The neoclassical building is gray brick with charming pediments over the first-story windows and doors and a balustrade around the roof. The county built a new courthouse (pictured) in 1991 that shares some of the same features such as columned porticos and balustrades on the roof. It is red brick and has three impressive arched window displays that tower over the wooden doors of the main entrance.

Glynn County is the seventh of the original eight counties created by the Georgia constitution in 1777. It was formed from St. David and St. Patrick parishes. The county was named for John Glynn, an English lawyer, member of Parliament, and a defender of colonial interests.

Liberty County

ADDRESS
100 North Main Street
Hinesville, Georgia 31313

YEAR COMPLETED
1926

ARCHITECTURAL STYLE
Neoclassical Revival

DESIGNER
J. J. Baldwin

MATERIAL
Brick

YEAR PLACED ON NATIONAL REGISTER
OF HISTORIC PLACES
1980

CURRENT USE
County Administration

The Liberty County courthouse in Hinesville was built in 1926. Two wings, extending from the core of the courthouse, were added in 1964. This courthouse has several superb features including a neoclassical portico, slender columns, and a stylishly domed clock tower.

Liberty County was one of the seven Georgia counties created from the original colonial parishes in 1777. The name for Liberty County was given based on the patriotic history of the parish from which it was created. St. John's Parish was the first parish in Georgia to vote for liberty from the British.

McIntosh County

ADDRESS
310 Northway
Darien, Georgia 31305

YEAR COMPLETED
1872

ARCHITECTURAL STYLE
Vernacular

DESIGNER
Unknown

MATERIAL
Brick

CURRENT USE
Courthouse

Built in 1872, the McIntosh County courthouse in Darien lacks the decorative flair that cloaked a number of Georgia courthouses in the late nineteenth century. The absence of an embellished style gives the McIntosh County courthouse a provincial charm, even with its modest additions and improvements over the years.

McIntosh County was created from Liberty County by an act of the state legislature in 1793. Its name honors the McIntosh family, whose members were among the earliest Scottish Highlanders to settle the area three years after Georgia became a colony.

Pierce County

ADDRESS
3550 West Highway 84
Blackshear, Georgia 31516

YEAR COMPLETED
1902

ARCHITECTURAL STYLE
Neoclassical Revival

DESIGNER
J. W. Golucke

MATERIAL
Brick

YEAR PLACED ON NATIONAL REGISTER
OF HISTORIC PLACES
1980

CURRENT USE
Courthouse

The Pierce County courthouse in Blackshear was built in 1902. The building's neoclassical portico has only two columns that support the pediment above it. The building has decorative pilasters that separate the building into bays of modest windows.

Pierce County was created from territory obtained from Appling and Ware Counties in 1857. It is named for Franklin Pierce, the fourteenth president of the United States.

Ware County

ADDRESS
800 Church Street
Waycross, Georgia 31501

YEAR COMPLETED
1957

ARCHITECTURAL STYLE
Modern–Stripped Classical

DESIGNER
William J. J. Chase & Associates

MATERIAL
Marble

CURRENT USE
Courthouse

Constructed of polished Georgia marble in 1957, the Ware County courthouse (pictured) in Waycross has a modern design. The main entrance has tall door and window panels with decorative panes in the windows. Pilasters frame its entrance and rise to a round pediment. This courthouse replaced the 1891 courthouse, which had earned the nickname the Castle for its medieval towers, spires, and large arched entrances.

Ware County was created in 1824 from Appling County. It has the distinction of being the largest county in Georgia. The county is named for U.S. Senator Nicholas Ware of Augusta.

GLOSSARY OF ARCHITECTURAL TERMS

Adapted from the *Georgia Courthouse Manual* (1992), produced by ACCG and the Georgia Department of Community Affairs and written by Jaeger/Pyburn Inc.

balustrade	A rail and the posts that support it (as along the edge of a staircase or balcony).
dormer	A window that projects from a sloped roof.
encaustic	A process in which a coloring agent is made to adhere to a surface by applying heat.
entablature	The three-part horizontal beam supported by columns (or seemingly supported by pilasters) in classical architecture. Divided into architrave, frieze, and cornice.
fanlight	A semicircular or semielliptical window above a door.
fluting	A series of vertical grooves on the shaft of a column or pilaster.
hipped roof	A roof with slopes on all four sides.
hood moldings	A projecting molding over a doorway or window.
keystone	The wedge-shaped stone at the top center of an arch that locks its parts together.
mansard roof	A roof with a steep slope rising to a separate gently sloped section on top. The lower section may be straight, convex, or concave in profile.
massing	The arrangement of the physical volume or bulk of a building.
parapet	The portion of an exterior wall that rises above a roof.
pavilion	A distinct section of a building, typically projecting from the walls of the main structure at its corners or in the center of a facade. Often covered by a separate or distinctive roof.
pediment	In classical architecture, the triangular space formed by the end of a gabled roof. Also, an ornamental surface framed by cornices above a door or window; normally triangular but occasionally arched or curved.

pilaster	A flat-faced representation of a classical column projecting from a wall.
quoin	An ornamental stone or brick on the outside corner of a building; may be load-bearing or simply decorative.
rehabilitation	The process of making possible a compatible use for a property through repair, alterations, and additions while preserving those portions or features that convey its historical, cultural, or architectural values.*
renovation	The process of repairing and changing an existing building for modern use, so that it is functionally equal to a new building; may include major changes.**
round arch	A semicircular arch.
rusticated stone	Cut stone with deeply recessed joints.
spalling	The fragmentation or shearing of the surface of brick or stone as a result of water penetration.
spandrel	A wall pane vertically separating the windows of a multistory building.
stringcourse	A projecting course of masonry forming a thin horizontal strip across a building facade. Often used to express boundaries between floors.

* Definition from the National Park Service.

** Definition from the *Dictionary of Building Preservation*, edited by Ward Bucher (New York: Preservation Press/John Wiley, 1996).

A NOTE ON THE TEXT BY GEORGE JUSTICE

This book is a showcase for courthouses in all 159 Georgia counties and provides certain historical facts and architectural features about them. It is not intended to be the defining resource of all things related to these courthouses. Rather, it is designed as a means of visually taking the reader on a teasing tour of one structural component that is representative of the rich culture found in the state's local communities. These courthouses are organized by a regional system developed by the Georgia Department of Industry and Trade in the 1980s. The choice to use this particular system was informed by the desire for both a practical guide for travelers and historical consistency. Each of the nine regions has interstates or major highways that connect the communities within it, thus giving the traveler an easy guide to its courthouses. Moreover, the counties in each region generally share some important connective histories that span from the first non-Native

Georgia settlers in the eighteenth century to the "new county movement" of the twentieth century. Finally, the regions often have common or similar natural geographic features such as the sandy plains, piedmont, and mountain counties.

The particular courthouses showcased throughout these pages are the result of deliberate decisions. In some cases, the pictures and text present a courthouse first built in the nineteenth century, such as the Banks County courthouse. For other counties, a twenty-first-century facility is featured, such as Whitfield County courthouse. The choices were made in an effort to demonstrate the variety of architectural styles that sweep the state's county seats and to contrast the diversity of development throughout the history of those courthouses that remain standing. Georgians in all counties possess their own particular civic pride that is reflective of their communities' uniqueness. The courthouses are symbols not only of that pride, but also of the very

sense of community created, in some measure, by the fact of the building's presence. The idiosyncratic selections offer a more accurate bird's-eye view of what Georgia was and is. The book, therefore, is not merely a historical look at Georgia's courthouses, but a tour in pictures and stories of the structural centers of the state's 159 counties.

Once I began to compile background materials for each of the planned Georgia courthouses, there was little doubt that this was something more than a book that highlighted the beauty of these historic buildings—it was a book that would concisely get at the retail, on-the-ground histories of local communities across the state. In all the years that I have taught Georgia history to college students, I had never encountered such rich stories discovered in the brick and mortar of these symbols of local governance. There was a language in both the style and substance of the courthouses that I only slowly began to fully appreciate. By the time I had finished, the text that I had contributed seemed pale compared to the pictures they supplemented. This is only appropriate, I think. My role, I came to conclude, was to relate just enough narrative detail for the reader to greater appreciate the communities that surround these buildings. It is the photographs and the material artistry of the buildings that truly tell the stories that words cannot.

For greater detail on all things Georgia, including many of the fascinating facts I have mentioned only briefly in this book, the reader would be well advised to consult the New Georgia Encyclopedia (http://www.georgiaencyclopedia.org). Without the gift of this public resource, much of the context and specific information contained in this book would have been much more difficult to access. The NGE, in fact, has been an invaluable tool as a means to quickly see into the lives of Georgia's people, communities, and cultures. It is certainly one of the most important contributions to a public understanding of the state's history in recent decades.

I would be remiss if I did not also credit the other, more exhaustive studies of courthouses and other general sources about Georgia counties that have been so valuable to my efforts in this project. Certainly, without them, this work would not have been possible. These sources include Wilber W. Caldwell, *The Courthouse and the Depot: The Architecture of Hope in an Age of Despair: A Narrative Guide to the Railroad Expansion and Its Impact on Public Architecture in Georgia, 1833–1910* (Macon: Mercer University Press, 2001); Robert H. Puster, *Courthouses in Georgia, 1825–1983* (Norcross: Harrison Co., 1984); Georgia Department of Community Affairs/Association County Commissioners of Georgia and Jaeger/Pyburn Inc., *The Georgia Courthouse Manual* (Atlanta: Georgia Department of Community Affairs, 1992); Ed Jackson, *Georgia County Courthouses* ("An Online Almanac about Georgia," 2000: http://georgiainfo.galileo.usg.edu/courthouses/contents.htm, last accessed November 25, 2013); and Georgia Humanities Council, *The New Georgia Guide* (Athens: University of Georgia Press, 1996).

ACKNOWLEDGMENTS

Courthouses of Georgia represents a project that was envisioned, developed, and produced by a team of individuals who collectively dedicated their time and talents to create a photography book that will leave a lasting impression on all that have an opportunity to turn its pages.

Thanks are first extended to the ACCG Board of Managers for endorsing this project as part of ACCG's centennial anniversary. These outstanding leaders are positively impacting the future not only of their counties but of our association, as well. ACCG also recognizes the role that elected county officials and appointed county staff played in helping to edit the fine details on their county courthouse.

ACCG executive director Ross King's passion for celebrating public service as well as his commitment to leaving a lasting centennial anniversary legacy is clearly realized through initiatives such as this courthouse book. ACCG communications director Beth Brown and Centennial project manager Deb Murphy put their expertise in organization and coordination to move this project from concept to reality.

Steve Nygren, the founder of Serenbe Community in south Fulton County, the home of Newington Photography, introduced Ross King to international photographer Greg Newington. This introduction led to further discussions—and the inspiration for a courthouse photography book was born. Greg focused his camera lenses on Georgia counties and captured the community spirit and uniqueness of their courthouses. This project also would not have been possible without Regan Williams, Greg's business partner, who scouted courthouse locations, organized photo shoots, and worked expertly with the University of Georgia Press and the ACCG staff behind the scenes on the many details of the book's production.

When Georgia Humanities Council president Jamil Zainaldin first saw the photographs for the book, his excitement for the project was immediate. Jamil facilitated the introduction to University of Georgia Press director Lisa Bayer and her staff and helped to spark their interest in the project. He also brought George Justice, the author of the book's text, to the project and assisted in proofreading several manuscript versions. ACCG appreciates its longstanding relationship with the Georgia Humanities Council and recognizes that this partnership will only grow as *Courthouses of Georgia* is released and serves as another resource for the New Georgia Encyclopedia.

University of North Georgia lecturer George Justice wrote the architectural sketches of each of the courthouses presented to help readers understand some of the details and history behind these remarkable structures. ACCG appreciates his attention to detail, willingness to work under extremely short deadlines, and flexibility through the editing process. Additionally, ACCG thanks Dr. David Crass and the staff of the Georgia Department of Natural Resources, Historic Preservation Division, for their review of the National Register listings, architectural styles, glossary, and other information presented in the book.

University of Georgia Press acquisitions editor Patrick Allen and project editor John Joerschke expertly guided ACCG through the book's review, approval, and production process. Their insight and experience kept the project on track. ACCG also thanks John Inscoe and Liz Lyons, who served as academic peer reviewers for the book and provided outstanding input based on their expertise. Additionally, ACCG thanks the University of Georgia Press editorial board for approving this project.

Last, but certainly not least, ACCG appreciates the involvement of our own professional staff and interns, who supported the production of *Courthouses of Georgia* from its earliest stages, through rounds of proofing and editing to its completion, including Randy Hartmann, Jim Grubiak, Kelly Pridgen, Michele NeSmith, Quint Robinson, Schuyler Harding, Carmenza Whitley, Natalie Fitzgerald, Kathy Nilsson, Rhonda Ligons, Eric Lopez, Amber Keller, Ren Yang, Grace Kim, Yterenickia Bell, Sarah Bangs, and Joanna Sanders.

ACCG, Georgia's county association, thanks the following for their support of the centennial of ACCG's work to ensure that Georgia's counties can provide the necessary leadership, services, and programs to meet the health, safety, and welfare needs of their citizens.